J I N R O N G

新时代金融风险与金融安全研究书系

中小企业负债
融资数量、利率与模式
创新风控研究

XINSHIDAI JINRONG FENGXIAN YU JINRONG ANQUAN YANJIU SHUXI

宋力源 张诚 王凤羽 著
宋力源 译

ZHONGXIAO QIYE FUZHAI
RONGZI SHULIANG 、LILÜ YU MOSHI
CHUANGXIN FENGKONG YANJIU

本书解释和论证后金融危机时代各国实施货币宽松，
而适度提高企业负债政策背后的原因，
以及在互联网社交网络环境下，
参与人如何融资模式创新以及如何进行系统风险防控?
力求从实践中去建议，
各国金融财政监管机构在经济下行的情况下，
应实施何种金融与财政政策。

Southwestern University of Finance & Economics Press
西南财经大学出版社

图书在版编目(CIP)数据

中小企业负债融资数量、利率与模式创新风控研究:汉英对照/宋力源,张诚,王凤羽著;宋力源译.—成都:西南财经大学出版社,2019.10
ISBN 978-7-5504-3930-6

Ⅰ.①中… Ⅱ.①宋…②张…③王… Ⅲ.①中小企业—企业融资—债务—研究—汉、英②企业经营管理—研究—汉、英 Ⅳ.①F275.6②F272.3

中国版本图书馆 CIP 数据核字(2019)第 073465 号

中小企业负债融资数量、利率与模式创新风控研究
宋力源 张诚 王凤羽 著
宋力源 译

责任编辑:植苗
装帧设计:穆志坚 张姗姗
责任印制:朱曼丽

出版发行	西南财经大学出版社(四川省成都市光华村街 55 号)
网 址	http://www.bookcj.com
电子邮件	bookcj@foxmail.com
邮政编码	610074
电 话	028-87353785
照 排	四川胜翔数码印务设计有限公司
印 刷	四川五洲彩印有限责任公司
成品尺寸	170mm×240mm
印 张	9.75
字 数	207 千字
版 次	2019 年 10 月第 1 版
印 次	2019 年 10 月第 1 次印刷
书 号	ISBN 978-7-5504-3930-6
定 价	68.00 元

序

在现代经济社会中，中小企业需要创新、需要技术进步、需要拥抱“互联网+”等，但是这一切的前提是需要资金，而资金的来源则主要有外源性融资和内源性融资两种。

融资与负债是一对孪生兄弟。中小企业融资的数量与负债的多少直接相关，而负债的风险又与利率直接相关。在金融资源相对不足或者融资渠道不畅的情况下，就需要金融创新，而进行金融创新就意味着不确定性即金融风险的产生，也就离不开对金融风险控制方法的研究。本书主要围绕以下几个问题展开论述：

（1）为什么中小企业需要融资和负债？本书第1章论述了企业负债融资对于企业经营利润的影响。通过对中国2002—2016年179个月份的工业企业成本费用利润率与资产负债率的数据采用对数一阶差分后协整检验通过后的回归方程和系统仿真分析发现：企业利润与负债具有长期稳定关系，且在短期内也呈现平稳时序趋势，企业利润率与资产负债率呈正相关关系，当期利润与前期利润正相关，合理的负债率增加可以提高企业的利润率水平，前期好的经营状况可以提高当期的利润率水平。研究结果表明，中小企业日常经营活动中需要适当负债。

（2）为什么中小企业负债融资具有风险？风险如何计量？中小企业负债经营活动中需要考量负债的风险，而负债的风险与负债利息水平直接相关，因而如何考量借贷利率风险的大小就是一个不能回避的课题。在中国中小民营企业的借贷利息风险的形成、发展、爆发等几个过程中，博弈的参与主体的信息往往是非完全的、非对称的，这在某种程度上增加了借贷风险积聚的可能性和突发性。因而本书第2章则利用贝叶斯博弈理论分析了社会网络关系下，中小民营企业民间借贷经济行为的利息根源以及风险防控的方法。

（3）中小企业融资负债的创新形式及风险表现是什么？供应链金融是中小企业融资创新的模式之一。闭环供应链金融是供应链金融的特殊表现形式，具有一定的代表性。本书第3章运用系统动力学理论，通过系统机制设计，把闭环供应链上独立的中小企业资金链有机地联系起来，并对系统进行机制设计前与机制设计后动态系统仿真的对比研究。研究发现：随着企业规模的扩大以及市场风险的加剧，中小企业闭环供应链上独立的中小企业资金链常常表现出一定的脆弱性，而中小企业闭环供应链金融系统则表现出较强刚性和协同性。

（4）中小企业融资负债的供应链金融创新模式及风险控制方法有哪些？供应链金融创新的主要模式有保兑仓、融通仓、应收账款三种。中小企业线上“保兑仓”是我国商业银行为了解决“麦克米伦缺口”而专门设计的一种金融创新产品。在本书第4章中，首先对我国商业银行“保兑仓”的主要应用流程以及应用模式进行了分解，进而构造了包括商业银行及供应链核心企业等多方博弈演化模型，通过数理推导，研究了线上“保兑仓”多方演化博弈的均衡解及其均衡点的稳定性，并描述了博弈的动态演化路径图。在此基础上，创新性地提出了“保兑仓”业务在一种非对称信息状态下信息迭代的方法——博弈视角下的主观贝叶斯测算方法，并进行了该方法的系统仿真设计，以帮助商业银行动态及时有效地控制该项金融产品业务的动态风险。最后通过基于Simulink的系统仿真设计及数值模拟测试证明了演化博弈及主观贝叶斯方法仿真系统的实用性和便捷性。

（5）中小企业如何借助定量的方法辨识风险点以及提前控制供应链上的信用证风险？在本书第5章中，针对目前我国出口企业对供应链上信用证结算风险评估和控制的难题，采用定量的方法，利用探索性因子分析的方法提取主因子。在此基础上，使用Vensim软件设计供应链上信用证系统动力学因果关系图和系统流程图，并构造各Dynamo参数方程组，通过系统仿真观测系统风险波动图，并针对供应链企业如何辨识风险点以及提前控制信用证风险给出建议。

以上即为作者及编译者就中小企业负债融资数量、利率与模式创新风险控制这一课题进行的一些探索性的研究。考虑到一些大学及研究生以上相关专业国际留学生可能需要阅读，该书内容采用中英文对照双语版形式撰写。当然，由于时间、作者和编译者水平的限制，本书中的缺漏、错误之处在所难免，不足之处还望各位专家、读者给予指正。

作者

2019年3月

目 录

Contents

1 适度负债论：工业企业负债率适度增加可以提高利润率水平吗？
——来自 2002—2016 年的时序数据证据

1.1 问题的提出

自从 2008 年美国次贷危机引发全球金融危机以来，加上近些年令人感到踌躇不安的“欧债危机”系列阵痛事件，人们对于公司负债融资经营利好的信任已经降到了最低点。一些国家商业银行和其他金融机构开始更加微观审慎地进行资产方管理，一些国外企业也开始对正常的负债经营感到不安。为了实现经济复苏，美国联邦储蓄委员会推出了“QE1 计划”，在公开操作市场买入政府支持企业债券以降低公司负债经营的违约风险；欧洲、日本也推出了“欧版 QE 计划”和“日版 QE 计划”，以降低债务违约风险。

一方面，2015 年国务院总理李克强在国务院常务会议上提出企业要降低融资成本和去杠杆率，中国社科院李杨研究员认为需要控制我国企业目前的债务水平。但另一方面，我国近两年采取了适度宽松的货币政策，央行几次下调了存贷款基准利率，2017 年 1 月份社会融资总规模达到了 37 377.03 亿元，有商业银行贷款规模为 23 132.85 亿元，达到了前所未有的高度。一方面去杠杆而另一方面增加企业债务融资规模，看似矛盾的做法内在的原因是什么呢？

我国不少地方政府、金融机构以及企业家对于企业负债经营的未来利弊感到疑惑：企业资产负债率的提高是否有利于企业经营利润的增加？为什么我国金融机构要为中小企业注入更多的资金流动性？要回答这些问题，就需要通过对宏微观企业经营数据进行统计分析来找出金融现象背后的原因和规律。

1.2 国内外相关文献综述

1.2.1 国外的研究文献

企业融资理论最早产生于 Modiglian 和 Miler（1958）推出的 MM 理论，在高度强假设条件下，MM 理论认为企业的盈利水平与企业的债务融资规模和融资结构无关。后来，在实践检验过程中，Modigliani 和 Miler 又对 MM 假设进一步增加了税收假设条件，论证了现实中债务融资的增加可以减少税收缴纳，从而提高企业的盈利水平。在此基础上，Stiglitz（1974）与 Smith 和 Warner（1979）释放了 MM 理论的破产假设条件，提出了债务融资权衡考虑理论，认为企业债务融资的增加可以提高企业的盈利，但是也可能引起企业破产。Wessels 和 Timan（1988）释放了 MM 理论融资途径假设条件，证明了现实经济生活中债务融资优先顺序的存在。随后 Jensen 和 Meckling（1976）释放了 MM 理论对经理人的假设，认为企业债务融资可以实现经理人与企业的目标一致性。Ross（1977），Leland 和 Pyle（1977），Myers 和 Majluf（1984），Stulz（1988）以及 Israel（1991）放松了 MM 理论的信息假设条件，证明了债务融资信息传递对绩效的影响。Heinkel（1982），Masulis（1983），Hpoitevin（1989）等通过对股票市场等数据进行实证研究，检验了债务融资水平对企业绩效的影响。

1.2.2 国内的研究文献

许家林、胡汇杰（2003），杨兴全、陈旭东（2004），吴昊、武央、邓宜康（2004），邵国良、王满四（2005），周振红、黄深泽（2006），吴春雷、马林梅（2007），郑瑞玺、徐新华、何青（2007），戴钰（2011），刘凤良、连洪泉（2012），穆玉堂（2013），宋小保（2014），何瑛、张大伟（2015），王希胜（2015），马红、王元月（2015），黄小琳、朱松、陈关亭（2015），朱佳俊、周方召（2017），陈涛、党兴华、贾窦洁、宋文飞、韩先锋（2017）等研究了企业债务融资、公司股权治理和企业绩效等几者之间的关系。

童盼、陆正飞（2005），张栋（2008），郭健、魏法杰（2008），龚光明、刘宇（2009），刘星、彭程（2009），吴海兵（2010），赵岩、王钧（2011），张琦生（2012），马娜、钟田丽（2013），赵岩、陈金龙（2014），胡援成、张朝洋（2015），彭程、刘怡、常欢（2017）等研究了企业负债融资与企业投资的相互影响关系。

陈建（2003），彭山（2003），刘莉（2006），李玉祥（2006），童丽珍（2007），杨华（2008），张宁（2008），王晶（2009），何俊琴（2010），孙继辉（2010），李玉玲（2010），王海强（2011），陈瑶（2013），蒋国平（2014），余海宗、陈文武（2014），李九妮（2015），叶明、李玉华、许硕磊（2016）等研究了企业的债务融资的财务杠杆、财务风险及其风险控制方法。

国内外学者在企业债务融资的研究上取得了不少的成果，一些研究成果是从博弈的角度研究；一些研究成果数据来源于A股主板市场或者创业板市场的微观数据，缺乏长时间跨度的国家宏观层面数据的支撑；还有一些研究成果是纯财务会计分析研究范式的。本书基于15年国家宏观经济统计数据进行分析，完善和补充了过去国内外的研究成果。

1.3 模型的研究设计

1.3.1 数据来源与模型设计

本书选取2002—2016年中国规模以上工业企业利润率以及工业企业资产负债率的月度统计报表，数据来源于中经网统计数据库，共选取15年的样本数据179个。由于数据呈现不规则波状分布特征（如图1-1和图1-2所示），故对于报表中个别缺省值采取就最近前期月份赋值处理。

根据企业财务管理的基本理论知识可知，企业当期的利润率不仅受到当期负债率水平的影响，同时也与当前市场环境决定下的前期利润率水平相关。因此，我们可以建立如下模型：

$$K_t = c + aL_t + bK_{t-1} + u_t \quad t = 1, 2, \cdots\cdots n \tag{1.1}$$

其中，L 为负债率，K 为利润率，a 为负债率系数，b 为利润率一阶差分后的系数值，c 为常数项，t 为时间。

1.3.2 回归模型的估计与检验

从图1-1、图1-2的时序图中我们可以看出，变量非平稳且存在着一定的相关关系，因而可以进行进一步的研究。首先为了消除异方差，对变量做了取对数处理，图1-3、图1-4为处理后的Quantitle-Quantitle图示。

本书利用Eviews 6.0经济数据统计软件，对非平稳时间序列进行单位根ADF检验。第一步对水平序列（level）进行三种选择检验：含漂移项（intercept）检验、含趋势项和漂移项（trend and intercept）检验、无附件项（none）

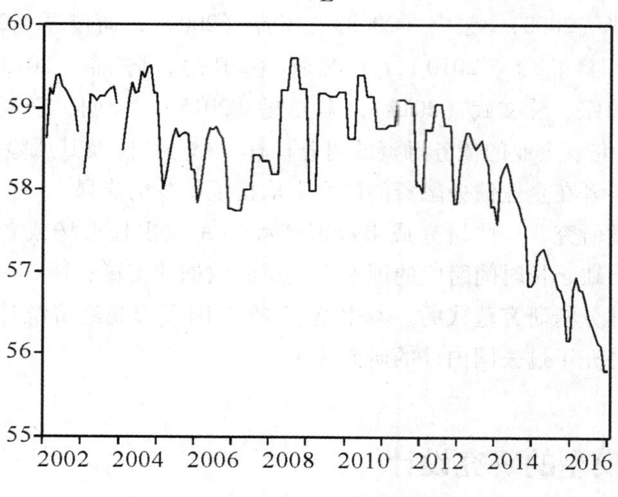

图 1-1　***L* 的线性趋势图**

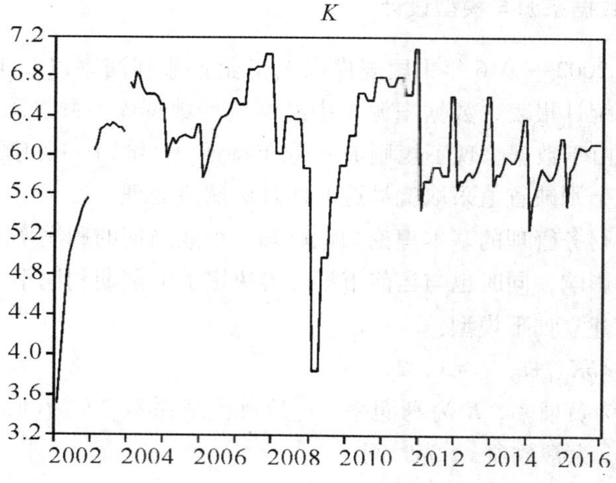

图 1-2　***K* 的线性趋势图**

检验，三种检验结果都显示 LN*k*、LN*l* 均为非平稳时间序列。以对 LN*l* 的 ADF 检验结果为例可以看出（表 1-1），ADF 的统计检验值为-0. 478 543，大于 10%显著水平的临界值-3. 145 341，相伴概率为 0. 983 6，远大于 0. 05，所以该时间序列是非平稳的。

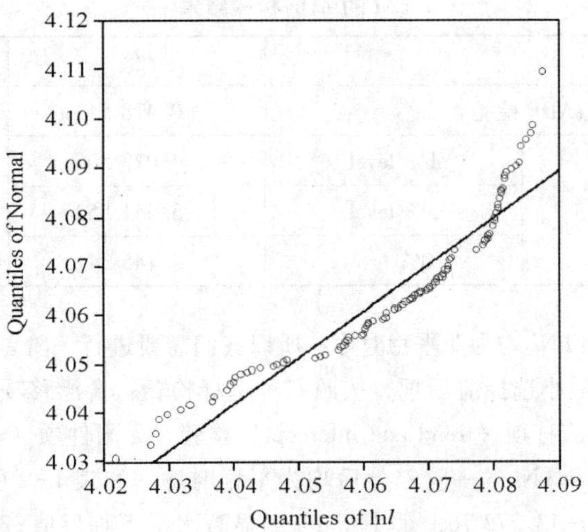

图 1-3　**LN*k* 与 Normal 分布的线性对比**

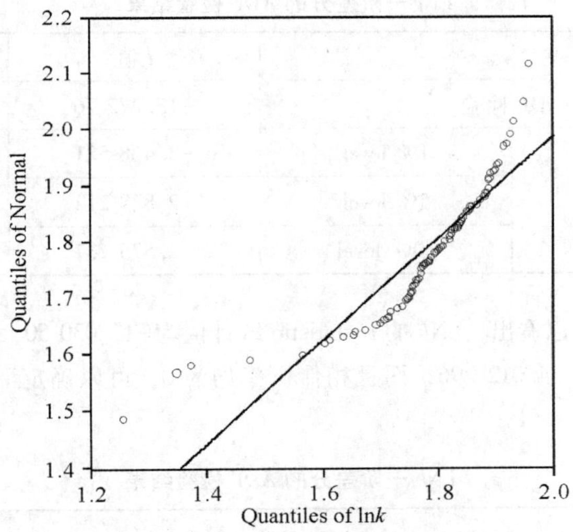

图 1-4　**LN*k* 与 Normal 分布的线性对比**

表 1-1　　LNl 的 ADF 检验结果

		t 值	p 值
ADF 检验		-0. 478 543	0. 983 6
置信水平	1% level	-4. 023 506	
	5% level	-3. 441 552	
	10% level	-3. 145 341	

由于 LNk 和 LNl 均为非平稳时序，所以我们需要进行一阶差分单位根检验。根据 AIC 和 SC 最小选择滞后项，按照三种选择检验：含漂移项（intercept）检验、含趋势项和漂移项（trend and intercept）检验、无附件项（none）检验。从结果来看，LNk 和 LNl 的一阶差分后均为平稳时序，如表 1-2 所示：LNl 的 t-statistic 统计值为-13. 272 76，远小于 1%的显著水平下临界值-3. 468 521，而且相伴概率均为 0，可以确定 LNl 为单整平稳序列。

表 1-2　　LNl 一阶差分的 ADF 检验结果

		t 值	p 值
ADF 检验		-13. 272 76	0. 000 0
置信水平	1% level	-3. 468 521	
	5% level	-2. 878 212	
	10% level	-2. 575 737	

从表 1-3 可以看出，LNk 的 t-statistic 统计值为-12. 030 50，远小于 1%的显著水平下临界值-4. 012 296，而且相伴概率均为 0，可以确定 LNk 为单整平稳序列。

表 1-3　　LNk 一阶差分的 ADF 检验结果

		t 值	p 值
ADF 检验		-12. 030 50	0. 000 0
置信水平	1% level	-4. 012 296	
	5% level	-3. 436 163	
	10% level	-3. 142 175	

从表 1-3 的 ADF 检验结果可知，中国规模以上工业企业资产负债率的自

然对数 LNl 为一阶单整序列，中国规模以上工业企业利润率的自然对数 LNk 为一阶单整序列。由于二者阶数相同，所以可以进一步作协整检验。打开 Eviews 的 Quick 按钮选择 Estimate Equation，输入含常数项的方程式和不含常数项的方程式，比较两种回归模型的估计结果，可以得到 LNk 和 LNl 的长期稳定协整关系方程。LNk 和 LNl 协整检验结果如表 1-4 所示。

表 1-4　　LNk 和 LNl 协整检验结果

	系数	t 值
LNl	0. 087 399	5. 599 48（0. 000 0）
LNk（-1）	0. 803 892	22. 850 8（0. 000 0）
R^2	0. 751 825	
调整后的 R^2	0. 750 390	
AIC	-3. 022 502	
DW	1. 939 894	

$$\mathrm{LN}k_t = 0.087\ 399\mathrm{LN}l_t + 0.803\ 892\mathrm{LN}k_{t-1} \tag{1.2}$$

$$\mathrm{ecm} = \mathrm{LN}k_t - 0.087\ 399\mathrm{LN}l_t - 0.803\ 892\mathrm{LN}k_{t-1} \tag{1.3}$$

1. 3. 3　残差估计与检验

为了保证模型的准确和精度，需要对残差 ecm 做进一步检验。对误差修正模型 ecm 作 Histogram-nomality test、单位根 ADF 检验、Corrogram-Q-Statistics，结果如图 1-5 所示。

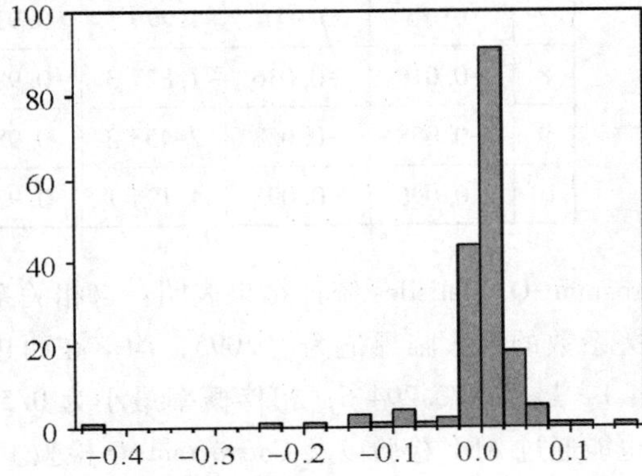

Series:Residuals	
Sample2002M032017M01	
Observations175	
Mean	-2.07e-05
Median	0.006 743
Maximum	0.163 078
Minimum	-0.429 545
Std. Dev.	0.052 932
Skewness	-3.928 071
Kurtosis	29.937 88
Jarque-Bera	5 741.226
Probability	0.000 000

图 1-5　**Histogram-nomality 残差检验**

从图 1-5 中可以看出，残差分布基本呈正态分布，误差修正模型的 Histogram-nomality test 检验的 Jarque-Bera 为 5 741.226，相伴概率为 0，大于显著临界值，因此 ecm 可以通过 Histogram-nomality 检验。

从表 1-5、表 1-6 可知：残差的 ADF 的 t-statistic 检验值为-2.243 612，小于 5%显著水平下的临界值-1.943 090，所以时序分布是单整的。

表 1-5　　残差的 ADF 检验结果

		t 值
ADF 检验		-2.243 612
置信水平	1% level	-2.581 349
	5% level	-1.943 090
	10% level	-1.615 220

表 1-6　　残差的自相关与偏相关检验

Autocorrelation	Partial Correlation		AC	PAC	Q-Stat	Prob
		1	0.041	0.041	0.294 6	0.587
		2	-0.031	-0.032	0.462 5	0.794
		3	-0.032	-0.030	0.651 2	0.885
		4	0.013	0.015	0.681 7	0.954
		5	0.068	0.065	1.524 6	0.910
		6	-0.013	-0.019	1.555 6	0.956
		7	0.035	0.041	1.779 5	0.971
		8	-0.016	-0.016	1.827 3	0.986
		9	-0.058	-0.058	2.453 3	0.982
		10	-0.096	-0.095	4.194 1	0.938

同时，延迟 10 阶后的 Corrogram-Q-Statistics 统计结果表明：自相关系数的最大临界值为-0.096，偏相关系数的最大临界值为-0.095，均落在两边的虚线范围内；Q 值最大为 4.194 1，最小为 0.294 6；相伴概率最小为 0.587，远大于临界值 0.05。因此 ecm 也能通过 ADF 检验以及 Corrogram-Q 检验。

1.3.4 回归模型的解释

通过对回归模型的估计与检验及对其残差的估计与检验可知，回归模型在长期和短期都存在稳定协整关系。

$$LNk_t = 0.087\,399LNl_t + 0.803\,892LNk_{t-1} \tag{1.4}$$

$$ecm = LNk_t - 0.087\,399LNl_t - 0.803\,892LNk_{t-1} \tag{1.5}$$

从上述回归模型中可知，利润率的对数函数 LNk_t 与负债率的对数函数 LNl_t 之间存在正相关关系，相关系数为 0.087 399，说明从短期和长期来看，工业企业在一定的合理区间可以提高资产负债率。也就是说，在风险可控的范围内，企业应该积极主动地进行负债融资，增加企业的现金流水平和运营活力，从而提高企业的经营业绩和利润水平。同时，LNk_t 与 LNk_{t-1} 之间的相关系数为0.803 892，说明企业当期的盈利水平与前期的盈利水平高度正相关，前期企业的经营状况会直接影响当期企业的盈利水平。

1.3.5 仿真数值模拟

根据工业企业负债率与利润率的回归方程，通过 Simulink 函数模块进行设计，并对该系统进行仿真运算，可以直观理解负债率与利润率之间的变动关系。

（1）假定工业企业负债率为斜坡函数，坡度为 0.5，负债率初始值为 0.3，T=10，可以得到如下仿真结果（见图 1-6 至图 1-8）：

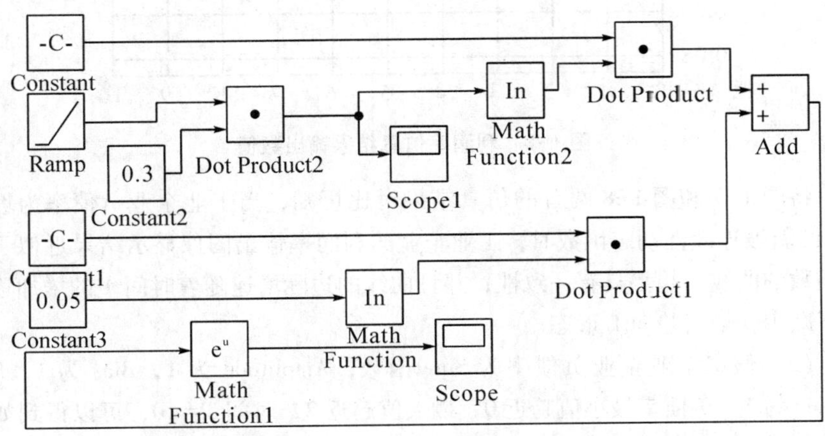

图 1-6 工业负债率为斜坡函数的仿真系统

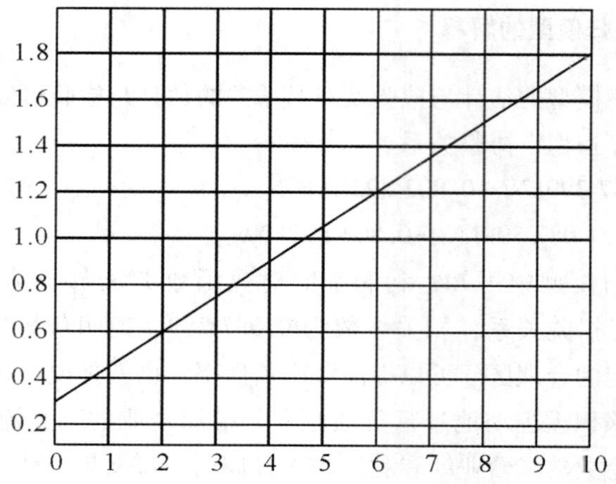

图 1-7　负债率为斜坡函数输入数值

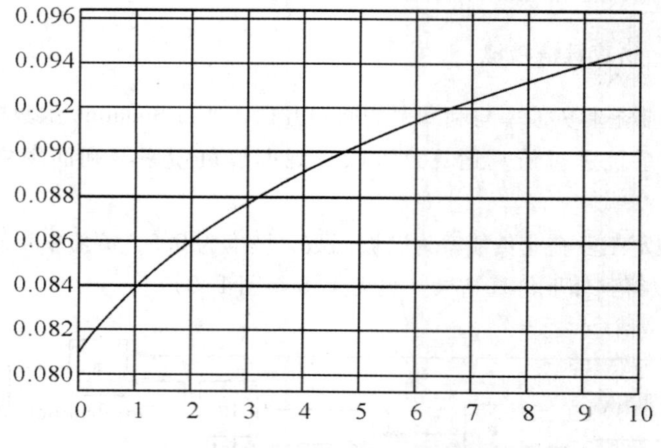

图 1-8　利润率仿真结果输出数值

将图 1-7 和图 1-8 两者的仿真结果对比可知，当工业企业负债率为坡度 0. 5 的斜坡连续性动态函数时，工业企业的利润率输出图像显示结果近似于斜坡函数的曲线，趋势具有一致性；并且曲线的边际增速随着时间 T 的增加逐渐向下减少，最后趋向 L 形态。

（2）假定工业企业负债率为 Sine 函数，Amplitude 为 1，Bias 为 1，Frequency 为 1。负债率最小值趋近 0，最大值趋近 2，时间 T=10，可以得到如下仿真结果（见图 1-9 至图 1-11）：

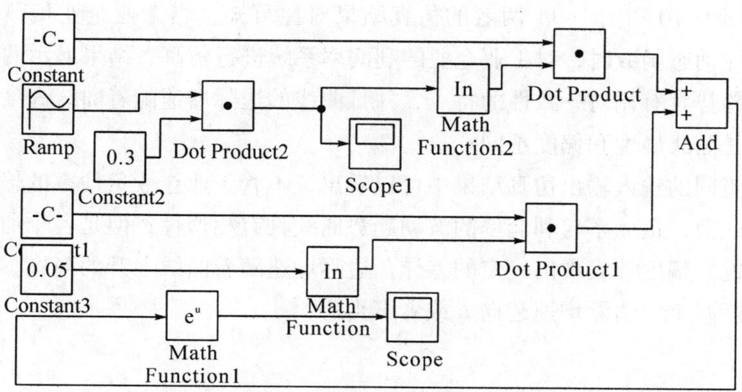

图 1-9 工业负债率为正弦波动函数的仿真系统

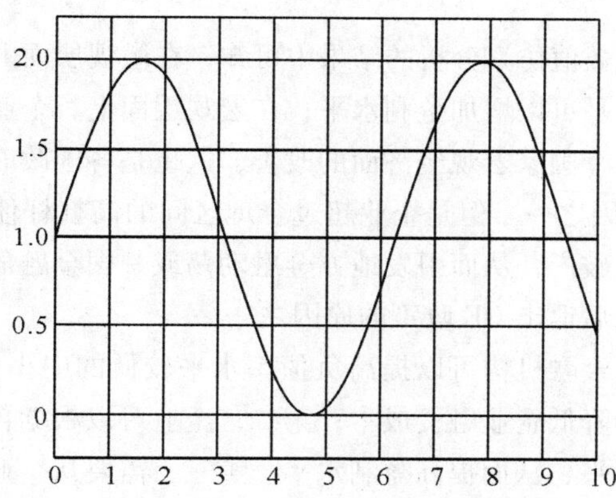

图 1-10 负债率为正弦函数输入数值

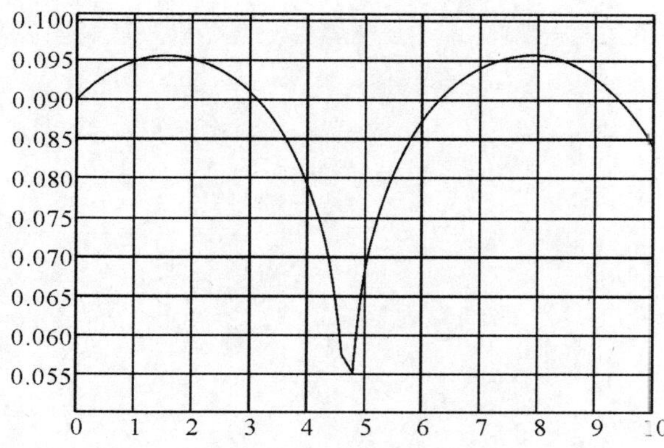

图 1-11 利润率仿真结果输出数值

将图 1-10 和图 1-11 两者的仿真结果对比可知，当工业企业负债率为正弦连续性动态函数时，对工业企业的利润率系统进行仿真，结果显示两条曲线的波动趋势具有相对一致性的特点，并且曲线的边际增速随着曲线高度不断减少，只是曲线峰度和偏度不同。

从不同的输入输出仿真结果中可以看出，不管工业企业负债率的输入值服从何种函数，负债率与利润率的波动趋势曲线具有相似性；但是各个曲线的坡度、峰度、偏度等表现出一定的差异，边际增速随着曲线上升的高度、坡度增大而不断减少，边际增速趋向 L 或者 V 形态。

1.4 研究结论

从函数回归及数值仿真分析的结果中可知，在微观层面上，企业在合理区间内提高负债率水平可以增加盈利水平；在宏观层面上，企业的盈利增加、企业繁荣可以引起整个国家宏观经济面的改善，这也是各国政府和中央银行竞先推出 QE 政策的原因之一。但是企业超过合理区间的高杠杆债务融资可能导致企业经营风险乃至破产，从而引发地方金融动荡或一国金融危机，这也是各国政府和中央银行先后退出 QE 政策的原因之一。

所以，第一，金融机构可以提高负债率水平较低的中小企业的融资水平，提高融资便利性和降低企业融资成本；第二，企业可以根据自身具体情况适度提高资产负债率水平，从而提高盈利水平；第三，需要从企业经营层面去控制财务风险，从而确保企业可偿债务在合理区间内运行。

1 Theory of Moderate Debt: CanModerately Higher Debt Rate Help Improve the Profit Level of Industrial Enterprises?

— with Evidence of Time-Series Data from 2002 to 2016

1.1 Introduction

With global financial crisis triggered by the 2008 U. S. subprime crisis, and the series of pain events, say, European debt crisis making people feel restless, the public's trust towards enterprise debt financing has dropped to the lowest point. Under this situation, in some countries, commercial banks and other financial institutions start to manage their asset side with a much more micro and prudential attitude, and some of the foreign enterprises also become uneasy about the normal debt operation. To achieve economic recovery, the U. S. Federal Reserve Committee launches the "QE1 plan", buying in the government supported enterprise bonds in the open market to reduce the default risks caused by the debt operation. Meanwhile, Europe and Japan also put forward "the European version of QE program" and "the Japanese version of QE program" so as to reduce the default risks caused by the debts.

In 2015, Chinese Premier Li Keqiang in the executive meeting of the State Council proposed that enterprises should de-leverage and reduce their financing costs. What's more, the famous economist and research fellow in Chinese Academy of Social Sciences Li Yang also believes that enterprises in China should control their debt level. However, the fact is that China has actually taken a moderately loose monetary policy in recent years, and the central bank also lowers the benchmark interest rate of deposit and loan several times: In January, 2017, China's total social financing scale achieved 3, 737.703 billion yuan, and its loaning scale in commercial banks was 2, 313.285 billion Yuan, reaching an unprecedented height. Are there any reasons for these two simultaneously adopted but seemingly contradictory approaches, say, de-leveraging on the one hand and increasing the enterprise debt financing scale on the other hand?

Many Chinese local governments, financial institutions and entrepreneurs are actually confused about the future pros and cons of the debt operation. Can improved debt asset ratio help increase enterprise profit? Why should Chinese financial institutions inject more liquidity into enterprises? To answer these questions, people need to find out the reasons and rules behind these financial phenomena through both the macro and micro analysis of the enterprise operating data.

1.2 Literature Review

1.2.1 Previous Studies outside China

Theory of enterprise financing first appears in MM theory put forward by Modiglian and Miler (1958). Under highly strong assumptions, MM theory holds that the enterprise profit level has nothing to do with the scale and structure of its debt financing. Later, in the practice-examine processes, Modigliani and Miler add the tax assumption (assumed condition of tax) to the MM assumption, and demonstrate that in practice increased debt financing can reduce the tax, and thereby can improve the enterprise profit level. On this basis, Stiglitz (1974) and Smith, Warner (1979) release the bankruptcy assumption of MM theory and bring about the trade-off theory of debt financing. They believe that the enterprise debt financing can either result in improvement of enterprise profit level or enterprise bankruptcy. Wessels and Timan (1988) releases the financing channel assumption of MM theory, and proves the existence of debt financing pecking order in real economic life. Still later, Jensen and Meckling (1976) releases the manager assumptions in MM theory, considering that by debt financing enterprises can achieve consistency in goals of the managers and the enterprises. Ross (1977), Leland & Pyle (1977), Myers & Majluf (1984), Stulz (1988) and Israel (1991) loosen the information assumption of MM theory, proving the impact of information transfer in debt financing on enterprise performance.

Heinkel (1998), Masulis (1983), Hpoitevin (1981) and so on demonstrate the impact of debt financing level on enterprise performance through empirical study of the data in the stock market.

1.2.2 Previous Studies in China

Xu Jialin, Hu Huijie (2003); Yang Xingquan, Chen Xudong (2004); Wu Hao, Wu Yang, Deng Yikang (2004); Shao Guoliang, Wang Mansi (2005); Zhou Zhenhong, Huang Shenze (2006); Wu Chunlei, Ma Linmei (2007); Zheng Ruixi, Xu Xinhua, Heqing (2007); Dai Yu (2011); Liu Fengliang, Lian HongQuan (2012); Mu Yutang (2013); Song Xiaobao (2014); He Ying, Zhang Dawei (2015); Wang Xisheng (2015); Ma Hong, Wang Yuanyue (2015); Huang Xiaolin, Zhu Song, Chen Guanting (2015); Zhu Jiajun, Zhou Fangzhao (2017); Chen Tao, Dang Xinghua, Dou JieJia, Song Wenfei, Han Xianfeng (2017) etc. research on the relationship among the enterprise debt financing, the enterprise equity governance and the enterprise performance and so on.

Tong Pan, Lu Zhengfei (2005); Zhang Dong (2008); Guo Jian, Wei Fajie (2008); Gong Guangming, Liu Yu (2009); Liu Xing, Peng Cheng (2009); Wu Haibing (2010); Zhao Yan, Wang Jun (2011); Zhang Qisheng (2012); Ma Na, Zhong Tianli (2013); Zhao Yan, Chen Jinlong (2014); Hu Yuancheng, Zhang Zhaoyang (2015); Peng Cheng, Liu Yi, Changhuan (2017) etc. explain the interrelationship between enterprise debt financing and enterprise investment .

Chen Jian (2003); Peng Shan (2003); Liu Li (2006); Li Yuxiang (2006); Tong Lizhen (2007); Yang Hua (2008); Zhang Ning (2008); Wong Jing (2009); He Junqin (2010); Sun Jihui (2010); Li Yuling (2010); Wang Haiqiang (2011); Chen Yao (2013) Jiang Guoping (2014); Yu Haizong, Chen Wenwu (2014); Li Jiuni (2015); Ye Ming, Li Yuhua, Xu Shuolei (2016) etc. discuss the financial leverage, financial risks and risk control methods in enterprise debt financing.

To sum up, scholars inside and outside China have made many achievements in terms of enterprise debt financing. Some researches have done their researches from the perspective of game; some others are micro data from A share main market or growth enterprise market, which lack support from long-span data on the macro national level; and most of the rest are research paradigms of pure financial analysis.

Thus, this study, based on a statistical analysis of 15-year macro economic data in China, aims to improve and supplement the previous researches both inside and outside China.

1.3 Model Design

1.3.1 Data Sources and Model Design

The data used in the research are from the monthly statistical reports of enterprise profit margin and enterprise debt asset ratio in China's large-capacity industrial enterprises (the annual main business income >= 20 million yuan) during 2002 to 2016. They are all obtained from the Database of China Economic Information Network, including 179 data samples of 15 years altogether. Since they take on an irregular wavy distribution (as shown in Fig. 1-1 and Fig. 1-2), data of the nearest previous month will be assigned to the very few default values in the report.

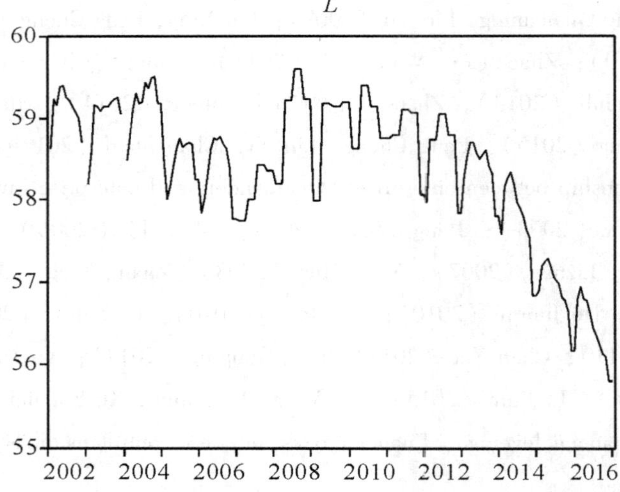

Fig. 1-1 Linear Trend Chart of *L*

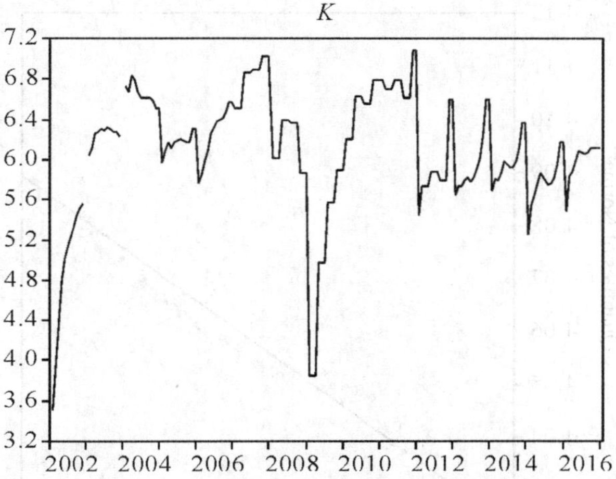

Fig. 1-2 Linear Trend Chart of *K*

According to the common sense of enterprise financial management, enterprise profit margin for the term is not only influenced by the debt ratio for the term, but also relevant to the profit margin for the previous term under the current market environment. Therefore, the model can be established as follows:

$$K_t = c + aL_t + bK_{t-1} + u_t t = 1, \ 2 \cdots n \qquad (1.1)$$

Among them, L (loan rate) stands for debt ratio, K (capital rate) for profit margin, a for the debt ratio coefficient, b for the coefficient after the first difference of the profit margin, c for the constant, and t for the time.

1.3.2 Estimation and Test of the Regression Model

From the time-series charts in Fig. 1-1 and Fig. 1-2 it can be seen that the variables are non-stationary and they correlate to each other to some extent, thus can be further studied. Firstly, to eliminate the heteroscedasticity, get the logarithm of the variables. Fig. 1-3 andFig. 1-4 are Quantitle-Quantitle charts after the logarithm processing.

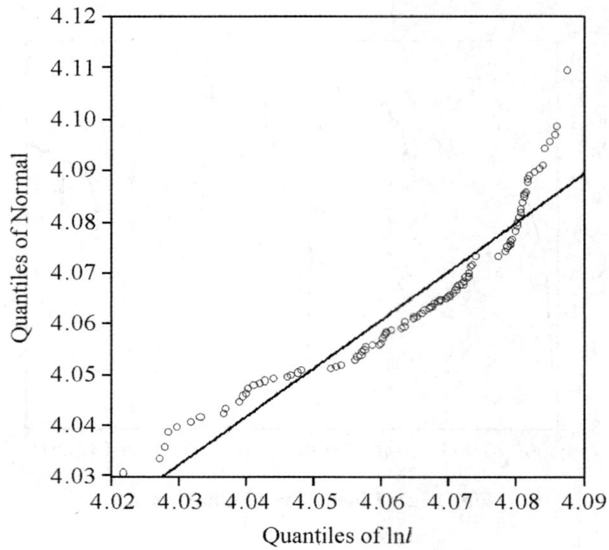

Fig. 1-3 LN*k* and Normal Distribution

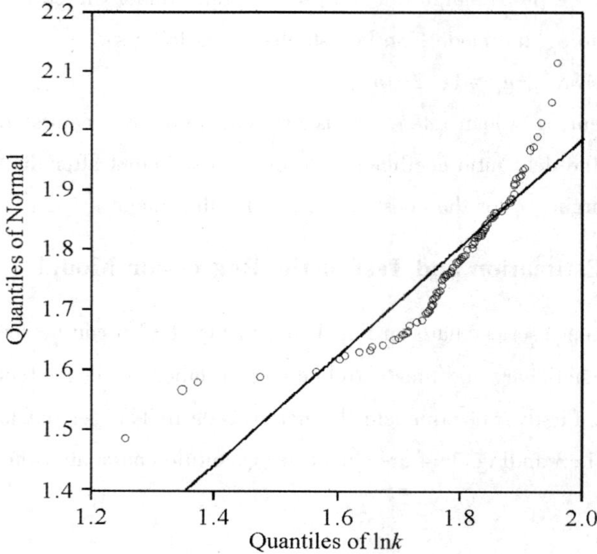

Fig. 1-4 LN*k* and Normal Distribution

With Eviews 6.0 (statistical software for economic data), apply unit root ADF test to the non-stationary time series. Apply one of the three test types to the level: intercept, trend and intercept or none test. Results of the three types of test all show that both LN*k* and LN*l* are non-stationary time series. E. g.: It can be seen from the ADF Test result of LN*l* (Table 1-1) that the value of ADF test is -0. 478 543, bigger than the critical value of -3. 145 341 at the significant level of 10%. The value P is 0. 983 6, much bigger than 0. 05. Thus, the time series is non-stationary.

Table 1-1 ADF Test Statistic of LN*l*

		t Statistic	*p*
ADF Test Statistic		-0. 478 543	0. 983 6
confidence level	1% level	-4. 023 506	
	5% level	-3. 441 552	
	10% level	-3. 145 341	

As both LN*k* and LN*l* are non-stationary time series, it is necessary to test unit root in first difference. Choose the optimal lag difference under the standard of making the values of AIC and SC smallest, and choose among the three test types: intercept, trend and intercept or nonetest. The resuts show that LN*k* and LN*l* after first difference are both stationary time series. As shown in Table 1-2: The t-statistic value of LN*l* is -13. 272 76, much smaller than the critical value of -3. 468 521 at the significant level of 1%. The value P is 0. Thus, it can be sated that LN*l* is an integrated stationary series.

Table 1-2 ADF Test Statistic of LN*l* after First Difference

		t Statistic	*p*
ADFTest statistic		-13. 272 76	0. 000 0
confidence level	1% level	-3. 468 521	
	5% level	-2. 878 212	
	10% level	-2. 575 737	

As can be seen from Table 1-3, the T-statistic value of LN*k* is -12. 030 50, much smaller than the critical value of -4. 012 296 at the significance level of 1%, and the value P is 0. The LN*k* can also be determined as an integrated stationary series.

Table 1-3 ADF Test Statistic of LNk after First Difference

		t Statistic	p
ADF Test Statistic		-12. 030 50	0. 000 0
confidence level	1% level	-4. 012 296	
	5% level	-3. 436 163	
	10% level	-3. 142 175	

It can seen from the ADF test statistics in the above tables that both LNl, the natural logarithm of the enterprise debt asset ratio in large-capacity Chinese industrial enterprises, and LNk, the natural logarithm of the enterprise profit margin in large-capacity Chinese industrial enterprises, are first integrated series (integrated of 1). The two are in the same order, so enabling us to further carry out the cointegration test. Press the [quick] button in EVIEWS, select the item [estimate equation], input equations either with a constant or without a constant, and compare the estimation results of the two regression models, and then we can get the long-term stationary cointegration equation of LNk and LNl.

Table 1-4 Cointegration Test Statistics of LNk and LNl

	coefficient	t test
LNl	0. 087 399	5. 599 48 (0. 000 0)
LNk (-1)	0. 803 892	22. 850 8 (0. 000 0)
R^2	0. 751 825	
Adjusted R^2	0. 750 390	
AIC	-3. 022 502	
DW	1. 939 894	

$$LNk_t = 0.087\,399 LNl_t + 0.803\,892 LNk_{t-1} \tag{1.2}$$

$$ecm = LNk_t - 0.087\,399 LNl_t - 0.803\,892 LNk_{t-1} \tag{1.3}$$

1. 3. 3 Estimation and Test of Residuals

To ensure the accuracy of the model, it is necessary to further test the residuals and the error correction model (ecm). Following are results of the Histogram-normality test, unit root ADF test, and Corrogram - q - statistics of the ecm.

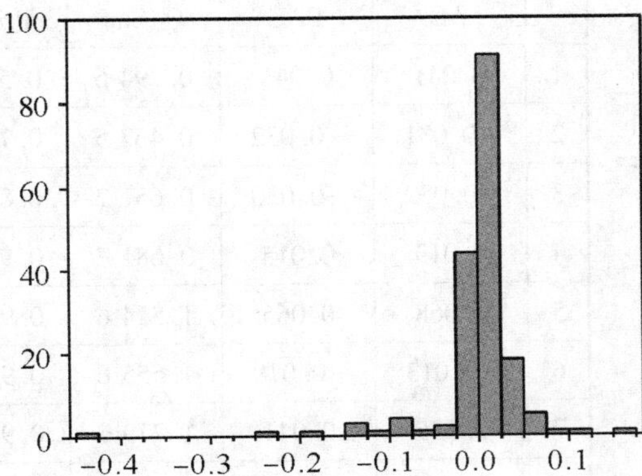

Fig. 1-5 **Histogram-Normality Test of Residuals**

From Fig. 1-5 it can be seen that the residuals take on a normal distribution, and Jarque-Bera value in its Histogram-nomality test is 5 741. 226, with value P of 0, which is significantly bigger than the critical value at the significant level. It means that the ecm passes the Histogram-nomality test.

Table 1-5 and table 1-6 show that the t-statistic in ADF test of the residuals is -2. 243 612, smaller than the critical value -1. 943 090 at the significant level of 5%. Thus, the time series is of integrated distribution.

Table 1-5 **ADF Test Statistic of Residuals**

		t Statistic
ADF Test Statistic		-2. 243 612
cconfidence level	1% level	-2. 581 349
	5% level	-1. 943 090
	10% level	-1. 615 220

Table 1-6 Autocorrelation and Partial Correlation Test of Residuals

Autocorrelation	Partial Correlation		AC	PAC	Q-Stat	Prob
		1	0. 041	0. 041	0. 294 6	0. 587
		2	-0. 031	-0. 032	0. 462 5	0. 794
		3	-0. 032	-0. 030	0. 651 2	0. 885
		4	0. 013	0. 015	0. 681 7	0. 954
		5	0. 068	0. 065	1. 524 6	0. 910
		6	-0. 013	-0. 019	1. 555 6	0. 956
		7	0. 035	0. 041	1. 779 5	0. 971
		8	-0. 016	-0. 016	1. 827 3	0. 986
		9	-0. 058	-0. 058	2. 453 3	0. 982
		10	-0. 096	-0. 095	4. 194 1	0. 938

At the same time, results of tenth Corrrogram-Q-statistics show that the maximum critical value of autocorrelation coefficient is -0. 096, while the maximum critical value of partial correlation coefficient is -0. 095. The two values are both located within the dotted line part on the two sides; the maximum value of Q is 4. 194 1, and the minimum value of Q is 0. 294 6; the minimum value of Prob is 0. 587, far greater than the critical value of 0. 05. Therefore, the ecm also passes the ADF test and Corrrogram-q test.

1. 3. 4 Interpretation of the Model

Through the estimation and test of the regression model and its residuals, it can be seen that there is a stationary cointegration relationship in the regression model in both the long run and short run.

$$LNk_t = 0.087\,399 LNl_t + 0.803\,892 LNk_{t-1} \quad (1.4)$$

$$ecm = LNk_t - 0.087\,399 LNl_t - 0.803\,892 LNk_{t-1} \quad (1.5)$$

From the above regression model we can see that the logarithm function of profit margin LNk_t positively correlates to the logarithm function of the debt ratio LNl_t, with a correlation coefficient of 0. 087 399. This indicates that from both a short-term and a long-term perspective, it is OK for industrial enterprises to moderately improve their debt asset ratios. That is to say, within the scope of controllable risks, the enterprise should adopt debt financing actively to increase the enterprise's cash flow and operation vigor, so as to improve the operating performance and its profit margin. At the same time, the correlation coefficient between $\mathrm{LN}k_t$ and $\mathrm{LN}k_{t-1}$ is 0.803 892. That means the enterprise profit level for the term highly correlates to its profit level for the previous term, and the operating performance for the previous term directly influence the profit level for the term.

1.3.5 Numerical Simulation Analysis

According to the regression equation of the debt ratio and profit rate of industrial enterprises, Simulink function module is designed. Then through the simulation analysis of the system, the changing relationship between the debt ratio and the profit rate can be intuitively understood.

(1) Assuming that the debt ratio of industrial enterprises is a ramp function, the slope is 0.5, the initial value of the debt ratio is 0.3 and $T=10$, the following simulation results can be obtained:

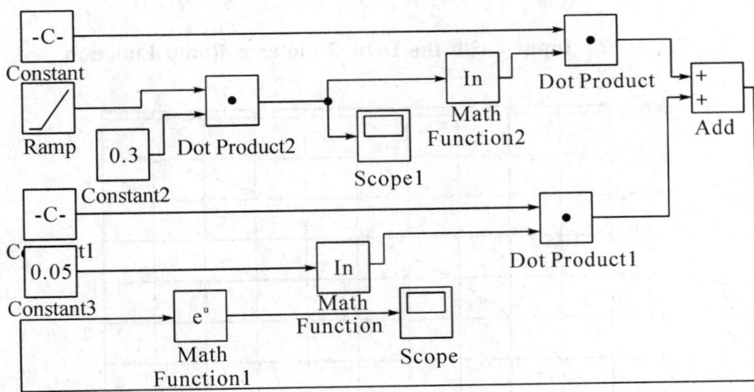

Fig. 1-6 Simulation System with Industrial Debt Ratio as a Ramp Function

Contrast between simulations in Fig. 1 - 7 and Fig. 1 - 8 shows that when the industrial enterprise debt ratio is a slope continuous dynamic function with its slope equaling to 0.5, the output curve of the profit rate in the industrial enterprises is similar to the curve of the slope function, namely, their trends are consistent. The marginal growth rate of the profit rate curve decreases gradually with time Tincreasing, and finally tends to L shape.

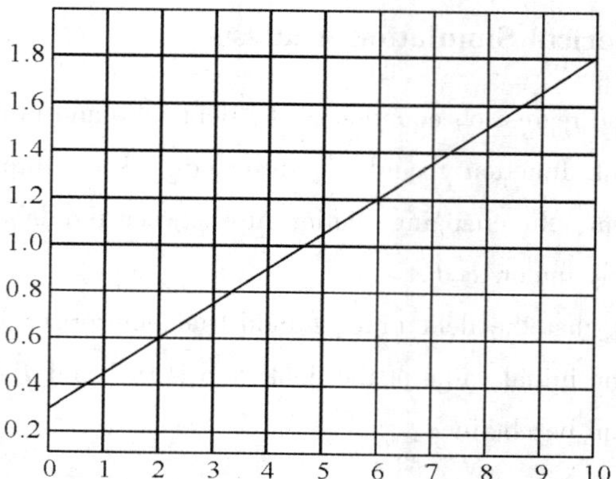

Fig. 1-7 Input: with the Debt Ratio as a Ramp Function

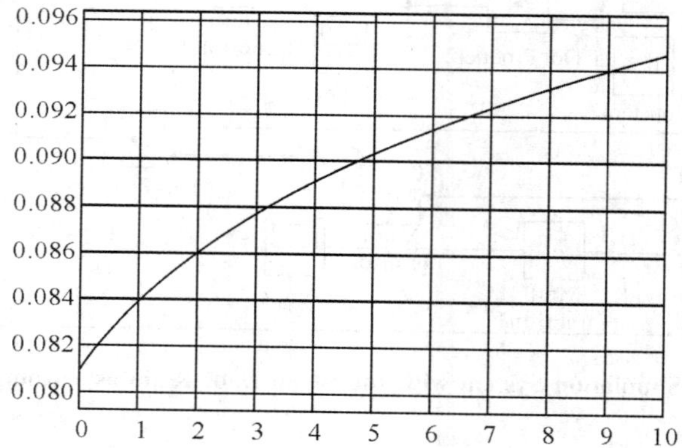

Fig. 1-8 Output: Simulation Results of the Profit Rate

(2) Assume that the debt ratio of industrial enterprises is a sine function, Amplitude is 1, Bias is 1, and Frequency is also 1. The minimum value of debt ratio is approaching 0, the maximum is approaching 2, time $T = 10$, we can get the following simulation results:

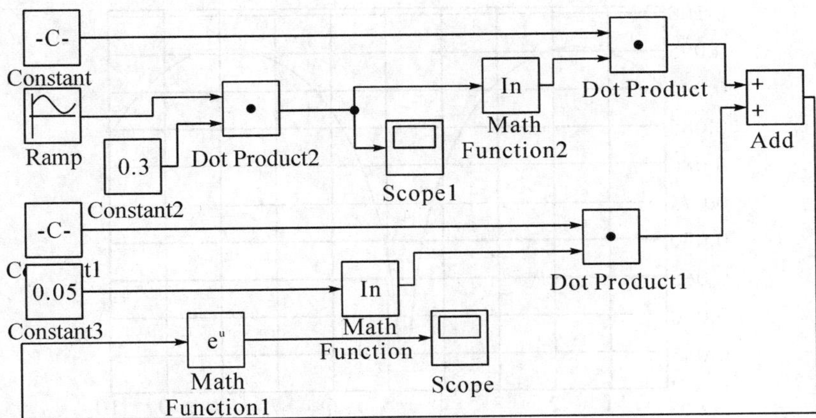

Fig. 1-9 Simulation System with Industrial Debt Ratio as a Sine Function

When the industrial enterprise' debt ratio is a sine continuous dynamic function, contrast between simulations in Fig. 1-10 and Fig. 1-11 shows that the fluctuation curve of its profit rate also tends to take on a relatively consistent shape. The marginal growth rates of the two curves decrease with the heightening of them, with the only difference lying in their kurtosise and skewness.

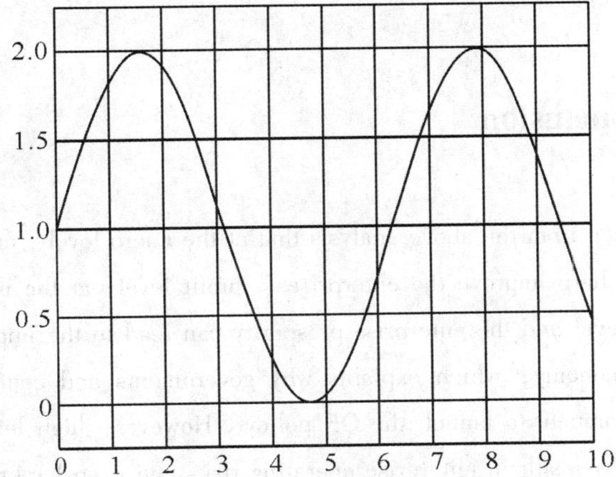

Fig. 1-10 Input: With the Debt Ratio as a Sine Function

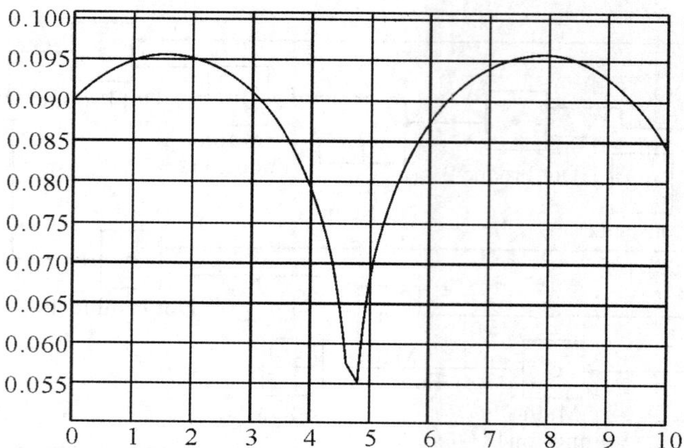

Fig. 1-11 **Output: Simulation Results of the Profit Rate**

It can be seen from the simulation results with different inputs and outputs that the fluctuation curves of the debt ratio and the profit rate tend to be similar no matter what function the input value of the debt ratio is. However, the curves show certain differences regarding to slope, kurtosis, skewness, etc. The marginal growth rates decrease with the heightening and the slope increase of the curves, finally tending to be the *L* or *V* shape.

1.4 Conclusion

It can be seen from the above analysis that at the micro level, moderate increase of debt ratio can help improve the enterprises' profit level; at the macro level, the improved profit level and the enterprise prosperity can lead to the improvement of the national macro economy, which explains why governments and central banks of so many countries compete to launch the QE policy . However, high leverage excessive debt financing may result in enterprise operating risks and even bankruptcy, possibly triggering crisis in local financial field or in a country, which is one of the reasons why governments and the central banks of some countries quit the QE policy.

Therefore, firstly, the financial institutions should further bring financing convenience and reduce the financing cost of those small and medium-sized enterprises with a relatively lower debt ratio, so as to help them improve their financing capability. Secondly, considering their own specific situations, enterprises can moderately raise their asset-liability ratio to increase their profitability levels. Thirdly, it is necessary to control the financial risks from the enterprise management level, so as to ensure that the enterprise's debt can run in a reasonable scope.

2 负债利率论：中小企业民间借贷利息价格博弈的研究

2.1 问题的提出

中小企业是现代市场经济体系中创新力较强、变革较快、扩张较快的经营主体。但在其发展初期，由于自身经济力量薄弱，中小企业需要从银行及其他金融机构进行借贷来满足自身的融资需求。然而，金融机构并不能完全满足中小企业这一迫切性需求。一份来自深圳市银监局的报告显示：13%的中小企业融资难度很大，57%的中小企业存在一定难度的融资问题。以温州为例，中小企业能够从主流金融机构获得贷款的比例只有10%左右，80%以上都是依靠民间借贷生存。浙江省台州市最大的民营企业之一飞跃集团因涉足高利贷而导致现金流枯竭，浙江省义乌市金乌集团董事长张政建出走，其原因也是高利贷引发的支付危机。因此，如何有效解决我国中小企业民间借贷风险问题成为当下一个比较热点的问题。

2.2 国内外研究现状

国内有关学者对这一现象进行了深入调查研究，比如张东琴、叶艺超（2011）认为我国外向型经济区对外贸依存度高，尤其是珠三角地区和长三角地区表现得极其明显。而中小企业受金融危机的影响，出口贸易遭受重创。陈大艳（2009）认为金融危机不断蔓延，而受到冲击最明显的是中小出口企业。陈宁、林汉川（2010）指出中小企业订单减少，利润大幅下降，成本大幅上升，造成大量的中小企业难以生存。郑熙春（2012）认为欧洲主权债务危机使我国企业对欧出口受到了越来越明显的冲击，外贸环境进一步持续恶化。

国外学者如 Tagoe N，Anuwa-Amarh E，Nyarko E（2008）研究了中小企业信息化管理和他们得到银行融资之间的关系，发现中小企业通过保持良好的信用记录和信息化水平可以提高他们融资的效率，而时代背景和产品类型等因素对获得确定融资作用甚微。Popescu，Cristian-Aurelia（2008）针对创新型中小企业的融资问题，研究了中小企业融资困难的主要原因，并提出了解决方案。Irwin D，Scott J M（2010）通过进行统计分析结果表明，企业家的种族、性别的差异对企业的再融资能力具有显著性差异，而他们所受教育的背景对融资能力的影响较小。Kundid A，Ercegovac R（2011）以克罗地亚共和国为例研究了金融危机背景下中小企业信贷配给的问题。

首先，以前许多学者是通过外部环境的变换、经济现象描述、法律制度规范来研究这一课题，对于参与主体的内在经济行为的根本动力的缘由未能做详尽的研究。其次，我国大多数学者只是从个体的层面对中小企业的借贷行为进行研究，未能从关系网络的相互影响、相互作用的角度来深入探讨。为了克服这些弱点，本书从网络关系下的微观贝叶斯博弈角度对中小企业民间借贷的经济行为进行分析。

2.3 民间资金出借人与中小企业民间借贷网络结构分析

资金出借人作为中小企业的民间借贷主体之一，并不是单独地做出博弈决策。在社会关系网络节点上每一个人都会不同程度地受到周围其他人的影响，从而不断修正他们原始的判断，我们可以通过图 2-1 的社会关系网络结构来分析说明这一问题。

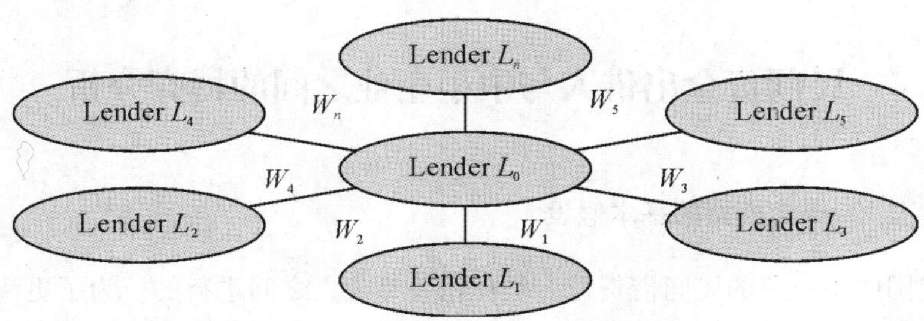

图 2-1　中小企业民间借贷的社会关系网络结构

模型假设：

（1）中小企业 A 的违约概率有一个先验违约概率 P_0，对于所有人来说是共有知识。

（2）出借人 L_0在做出借款之前会向其他人（熟人、朋友）咨询借款的风险大小，他又会受到其他人 L_1，L_2，……L_n的影响，从而进一步修正他的先验判断。

（3）假设参与人 L_1，L_2，……L_n互不相容，他们掌握的关于企业 A 的可能违约证据分别为 E_1，E_2，…E_n。LS_1代表 L_1根据证据 E_1成立时判断企业 A 违约的强度，$\mathrm{LS}_1=P(E_1/L_0)/P(E_1/-L_0)$。$\mathrm{LS}_1$越大，说明证据支持违约结论；相反，$\mathrm{LS}_1$越小，证据越不支持。$\mathrm{LN}_1$代表证据 E_1 不成立时判断企业 A 违约的强度。同理（LS_2，LN_2），……（LS_n，LN_n）亦是如此。

所以当自然人 L_0向 L_1咨询的时候，L_1根据证据 E_1判断告知 L_0他的判断，可算出 $\mathrm{LS}_1=P(E_1/L_0)/P(E_1/-L_0)$。$L_0$根据 LS_1会修正先验概率 P_0的大小，根据主观贝叶斯公式可以求得出借人 L_0的后验违约概率为：

$$P_1=P(L_0/E_1)=\mathrm{LS}_1\cdot P_0/[(\mathrm{LS}_1-1)P_0+1] \tag{2.1}$$

当自然人 L_0继续向 L_2咨询的时候，也会修正先验违约概率 P_0的大小，那么可以求得后验违约概率为：

$$P_2=P(L_0/E_2)=\mathrm{LS}_2\cdot P_0/[(\mathrm{LS}_2-1)P_0+1] \tag{2.2}$$

同理，向 Ln 咨询的后验违约概率为：

$$P_n=P(L_0/E_n)=\mathrm{LS}_n\cdot P_0/[(\mathrm{LS}_n-1)P_0+1] \tag{2.3}$$

假设在 L_0的社会关系网络中 E_1，E_2，……E_n的信用权重为 W_1，W_2，……W_n，则可得综合后验概率：

$$P_t=W_1\cdot P_1+W_2\cdot P_2\cdots\cdots+W_1\cdot P_n \tag{2.4}$$

其关系图请参考图 2-1 和图 2-2 所示。

2.4 民间资金出借人与中小企业之间的博弈分析

2.4.1 博弈模型的基本假设

我国中小企业的民间借贷行为是在相关参与人之间进行的，为了更清楚地分析问题和简化模型，我们对中小企业民间借贷博弈做出以下假设：

假设 1：贝叶斯博弈的双方参与人，包括中小企业、民间出借人都是完全理性的，即他们的经济行为总是从自身利益最大化的角度出发，这是每个参与

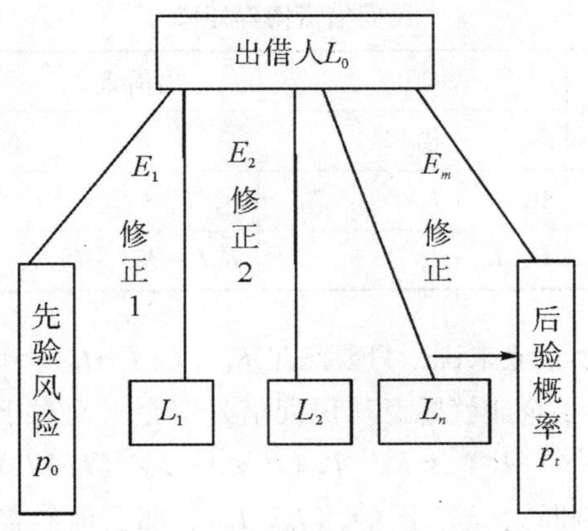

图 2-2　中小企业民间借贷的模型假设

人的共同特点，也是共同知识。

假设 2：参与人各方均不能获得对方的策略选择、收益函数以及参与人特征的完全信息，只能获得完美信息；对于博弈过程的了解是非对称信息，不能完全知道对方的博弈行为。

假设 3：博弈类型分为单人贝叶斯博弈和网络结构下多人贝叶斯博弈，分别用以描述博弈者的单个人或者多个人的不同理性决策过程。在单次静态博弈中，博弈人是根据当前的已知信息做出判断；而多次重复博弈是通过博弈参与人的相互作用来影响对在未来时间 t（一个月、一季度、一年内等）内总收益值的判断而做出的博弈选择。

2.4.2　民间借贷中民间出借人与中小企业间的贝叶斯博弈过程

（1）如果是一次性偿还本金的合约，我们忽略时间 t 对博弈双方的影响，只考虑博弈双方在一个简单单次博弈环境中进行选择。

第一步：假设民间出借人 A 对自有资金 K_0的策略空间只有两种选择：一是将资金 K_0存入银行或者其他投资机构，获得固定利息均值为 I_0的无风险性收入；二是将资金 K_0出借给中小企业，可以获得浮动利息 I_0+I_1的有风险性收入。

第二步：假设中小企业利用该部分资金 K_0去投资房产或者其他实业可以获得 I_X的收益率，那么我们可以通过以下的博弈矩阵（表 2-1）来刻画中小企业与出借人 A 的博弈选择：

表 2-1　　　　　　　　　　**民间借贷博弈矩阵**

中小民营企业	出借人	
	借贷	不借贷
不借贷	0，$K_0 \cdot I_0$	0，$K_0 \cdot I_0$
借贷	0，$K_0 \cdot I_0$	$K_0I_x - K_0I_1 - K_0I_0$，$K_0I_0P_t + K_0P_tI_1$

所以，对于中小企业来说，只要满足 K_0（$I_x - I_1 - I_0$）>0，即未来期望收益率 $I_x > I_1 + I_0$，那么中小企业就愿意从民间借入资金。而对于出借人来说，只要满足：K_0（$I_0 + I_1$）·（$1 - P_t$）$\geqslant K_0 \cdot I_0$（$P_t \leqslant 1 - I_0 /$（$I_0 + I_1$）），即出借人对中小企业的后验概率判断大于等于 $I_0/$（$I_0 + I_1$），那么他们将愿意将资金借出给中小企业；否则会将资金存入银行或者用于其他收益性金融投资。

简单单次静态贝叶斯的纳什均衡解为：{K_0（$I_x - I_1 - I_0$），K_0（$I_0 + I_1$）· P_t}，即在均衡条件下，中小企业可以获得 K_0（$I_x - I_1 - I_0$）的总收益，收益率为 $I_x - I_1 - I_0$，民间出借人可以获得 K_0（$I_0 + I_1$）·（$1 - P_t$）的收益，收益率为（$I_0 + I_1$）·（$1 - P_t$）.

（2）如果是多阶段付息合约，考虑时间 t 对于博弈双方的影响，那么博弈双方的受益值和博弈策略将会做出进一步调整。

首先，由于时间 t 的存在，博弈人在获得前期博弈结果后，会通过关系网络结构修正其后验概率判断。

根据图 2-2 显示，如果任意资金出借人 L_n 在时间 t 内成功获得利息收入，那么出借人 L_n 在 $t+1$ 阶段就会对中小企业的违约概率判断做出改变。比如 L_1 在 t 时间段对中小企业违约概率的判断是 $P(L_1)_t = 0.5$，由于 L_1 在 t 时间段成功地获得了（不能获得）利息回报，那么他（她）在 $t+1$ 阶段的对守信（不违约）概率判断会提升（下降），$P(L_1)_{t+1} > 0.5$ 或者 $P(L_1)_{t+1} < 0.5$。由于 L_n 阶段的改变和关系网络的影响，对于 $t+1$ 阶段即将进入民间借贷的出借人 A 的后验概率判断会做出进一步修改，从而改变任意出借人 A 是否进入民间借贷的博弈之中。这也是我们通过中小企业民间借贷现象可以看到的在不同的时期，总有一些借贷参与人在不断地进入或者退出博弈的根本原因。

其次，由于时间 t 的存在，博弈双方的收益值将会发生变化。根据表 2-1 显示，在新的博弈中加入时间参数 t。对于中小企业来说，在 t 时间段的期望收益值为：

$$G_0 = K_0 (I_x - I_1 - I_0)^t \tag{2.5}$$

对于民间借贷的出借人来说，在 t 阶段的期望收益值为：

$$G_t = K_0 \left[1 + (I_0 + I_1)\right]^t \cdot (1 - P_{t+1}) \tag{2.6}$$

所以对于民间借贷的出借人来说，愿意借出资金的条件也发生了改变，需要满足：

$$K_0 \left[1 + (I_0 + I_1)\right]^t \cdot (1 - P_{t+1}) > K_0 \cdot (1 + I_0)^t \tag{2.7}$$

解上式得到：$P_{t+1} < 1 - \left[(1 + I_0) / (1 + I_0 + I_1) \right.$

因而我们可以看出，随着时间 t 的变化，分母 $1 - \left[(1 + I_0) / (1 + I_0 + I_1) \right]^t$ 的值越大，民间资金出借人对于违约概率 P_{t+1} 的要求更高一些。而 P_{t+1} 的大小是受到上一阶段，即第 t 阶段中小企业守信程度对关系网络结构的影响。所以，中小企业如果想要长期成功获得民间借贷资金，需要对每一个阶段的上一阶段诚信守约，以增加守信概率 $1 - P_{t+1}$ 的值的大小，当 $P_{t+1} > 1 - \left[(1 + I_0) / (1 + I_0 + I_1) \right]^t$ 时，就会出现诉讼等纠纷。

2.4.3 案例分析

一家高科技公司进行民间借贷融资，为年利率15%，借款期限为5年，每年返还利息。该企业信誉一般，先验违约概率为30%左右。王女士从亲友那儿得知这一消息，并分别向比较熟悉这一领域的人 L_1、L_2 和 L_3 咨询这一民间借贷的风险事宜，他们告知王女士这一民间借贷的风险违约判断（LS_1，LN_1），（LS_2，LN_2），（LS_3，LN_3）的大小分别为（3，1）、（1.5，1.5）和（5，1）。那么通过网络结构分析，可以得到：

$P_1 = LS_1 \cdot P_0 / \left[(LS_1 - 1) P_0 + 1 \right] = 0.375$

$P_2 = LS_2 \cdot P_0 / \left[(LS_2 - 1) P_0 + 1 \right] = 0.13$

$P_3 = LS_2 \cdot P_0 / \left[(LS_2 - 1) P_0 + 1 \right] = 0.67$

因此，王女士认为其社会关系网络中的信用权重为：

$W_1 = 0.2$，$W_2 = 0.5$，$W_3 = 0.3$

王女士由此可判断出综合后验概率为：

$P_t = W_1 \cdot P_{t1} + W_2 \cdot P_{t2} \cdots\cdots + W_1 \cdot P_{tn} = 0.375 \times 0.2 + 0.13 \times 0.5 + 0.67 \times 0.3 = 0.341$

（1）如果是单次博弈，一次性偿还本金的合约，银行五年期的无风险年利率为7%，王女士通过博弈计算：$I_0 / (I_0 + I_1) = 0.07/0.22 = 0.32$，而 $P_t = 0.341$。

根据公式：只要 $P_t < 1 - I_0 / (I_0 + I_1)$，那么王女士就可以借出资金。

对于中小企业来讲，当收益率 $I_X - I_1 - I_0 > 0$ 时，才可以借入资金，即 $I_X > 22\%$。

（2）如果是多次重复博弈，多阶段付息合约，王女士则需要分以下情形做出决策：

如果企业在一年内没有按期支付利息，那么当 $P_{t+1}<1-[(1+I_0)/(1+I_0+I_1)]^t$ 时，为可以接受合约，而当 $P_{t+1}>1-[(1+I_0)/(1+I_0+I_1)]^t$ 时，就可能会出现失约或者法律纠纷。

如图 2-3 所示，$F(t)=1-[(1+I_0)/(1+I_0+I_1)]^t$，$F(t)$ 随着时间 t 的增加逐渐趋近于 1；同时，如图 2-4 所示，随着时间 t 的增加 P_{t+1} 的值则逐渐趋近于 0，两条曲线的交点为决策的临界点。当资金出借方面临交点的左方情形时，$P_{t+1}>1-[(1+I_0)/(1+I_0+I_1)]^t$，资金风险较大；当在交点的右方时，$P_{t+1}>1-[(1+I_0)/(1+I_0+I_1)]^t$，风险较小，可以借出资金。

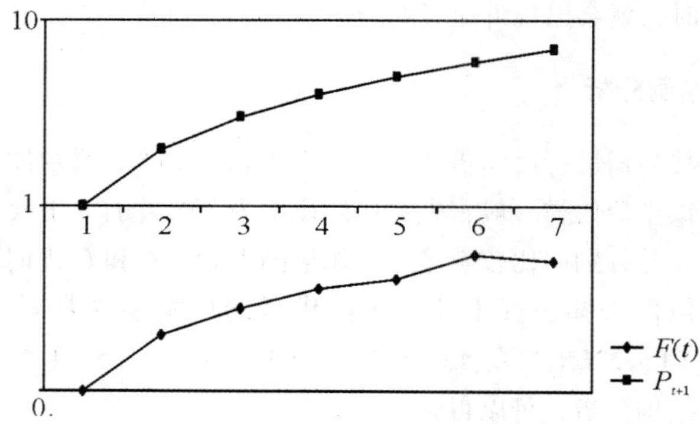

图 2-3　重复博弈动态变化

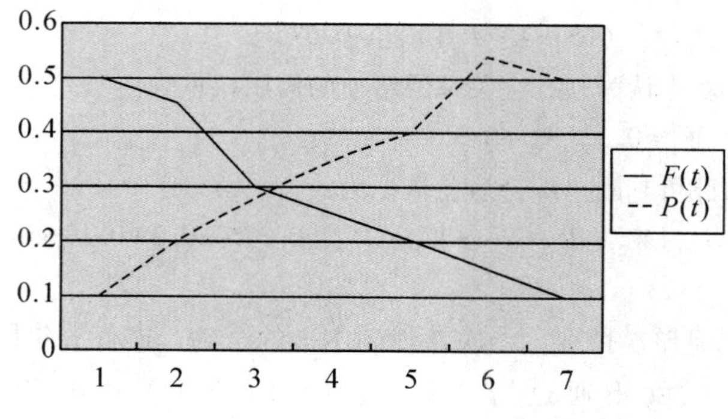

图 2-4　重复博弈动态均衡

2.5 对策与建议

通过上述分析可知，要解决信息不对称、民间借贷风险高、中小企业融资难、融资成本高的问题，可以从以下几个方面进行改进：

（1）应该拓宽中小企业的融资渠道，成立或组建更多适合中小企业融资的贷款银行或中小企业贷款担保机构，这样依靠正规的信贷渠道可以让大部分的中小企业的民间借贷行为分流或消失，而且正规的融资渠道对借贷双方的信用评价更加科学，会使得信用风险概率 P_t 更低，违约的经济成本更小。

（2）组建中小企业民间借贷的第三方服务机构来进行专业信用风险评估服务。参与人对 LS_1，LN_1 的评估往往强烈地带上了个人的主观色彩，容易让中小企业民间借贷双方对风险低估或者高估，很难做到客观公正地评价，而第三方服务机构正好能够克服这一缺点。而且第三方服务机构往往有专业的信息调查人员和信息服务网络，使得其对中小企业的经营模式、成长、业绩、还贷清偿能力等信息有更准确的把握，从而降低借贷风险，提高中小企业民间借贷的效率，同时也可以在某种程度上避免中小企业民间借贷的“道德风险”和“柠檬市场”的盛行。

（3）对中小企业的民间借贷行为进行一定程度的监管，以避免欺诈的出现。政府应通过充分论证出台一系列的法律法规来规范民间借贷市场，明确划定合法和违法资金以及合法借贷和非法高利贷之间的界限。同时政府还应成立专门的民间借贷督导小组，专门负责对民间借贷行为的规范服务，做到同时对资金出借人、中小企业以及第三方服务机构的安全监管。

2.6 结论

总之，中小企业的民间借贷过程涉及众多的参与者和方方面面。没有哪一个参与者能够不受到复杂网络的影响。也就是说，所有的理性决策都是在各种因素的影响下做出的。因此，要理顺和规范中小企业的民间借贷行为，首先要做的就是从微观角度分析中小企业的理性选择和决策行为。我们应把握事物的本质，提高中小企业借贷的信用水平，保障双方的合法权益，只有这样才能有效地规范和引导中小企业借贷，实现中小企业的长期健康发展。

2 On Interest Rate of Debt: Research on Games of SME's Private Borrowing Interest

2.1 Introduction

Small and medium-sized enterprise (SME) is one of the business forces with strong innovative power, rapid changing capability and fast expansion speed in modern market economy. But at the very beginning of their development, because of comparatively weak economic strength, SMEs need to loan from banks and other financing institutions so as to meet their own needs. Unfortunately, these needs can not always be fully satisfied by those formal financial institutions. A report from the China Banking Regulatory Commission Shenzhen Office shows: 13% of the SMEs face great difficulties in their financing processes, and other 57% of them also face certain difficulties. In Wenzhou, for example, only about 10% of its SMEs can obtain loans from the mainstream financial institutions, with other 80% of them relying on private borrowing for survival. Fei Yue Group, one of the largest privately owned enterprises in Taizhou, Zhejiang Province, China, encounters a depletion of its cash flow because of involvement in usury; the running away of Zhang Zhengjian, president of the Jin Wu Group in Yiwu, Zhejiang Province, China, is also caused by payment crisis triggered by usury. Thus, how to effectively solve the problem of SMEs' private borrowing risks has become a hot issue in China currently.

2.2 Literature Review

Some Chinese scholars have conducted in–depth investigations into this phenomenon. Zhang Dongqin, Ye Yichao (2011) thinks that China's export–oriented economic zones depend highly on foreign trade, especially the Pearl River Delta and the Yangtze River delta regions. And, influenced by the global financial crisis, China's SMEs are apt to be hit hard in their exports. Chen Dayan (2009) believes that with financial crisis spreading, it is the SMEs that have suffered the most. Chen Ning, Lin Hanchuan (2010) points out that with less orders, sharply decreased profits, and steadily rising cost, a large number of SMEs are struggling in their survival. Zheng Xichun (2012) holds that there is a more and more obvious impact of the European sovereign debt crisis on SMEs' exports to Europe, causing a further deteriorated foreign trade environment for China.

Scholars outside China such as Tagoe N, Anuwa – Amarh E and Nyarko E (2008) analyzes the relationship between SME s' information management and their access to bank financing. It is found that SME can improve its financing efficiency by keeping a good credit record and a high information level. However, factors such as the background of the times and product types have little effect on obtaining financing. Targeting at the financing problems of innovative SME, Popescu and Cristian–Aurelia (2008) not only elucidates on the main reasons for SMEs' financing difficulties but also offer some suggestions. What's more, the results of Irwin D and Scott J M (2010) 's statistical analysis idicates that the differences in races and genders of entrepreneurs have significant influence on the refinancing capability of enterprises, whereas their educational background has little influence. Furthermore, taking the Republic of Croatia as an example, Kundid A, Ercegovac R (2011) discusses the credit rationing of SMEs in the context of the financial crisis.

From above we can see: firstly, many scholars before have discussed this subject from various perspectives such as changes of external environment, description of economic phenomena, and regulation of legal system. However, they have hardly traced the root causes for the economic behaviors of those participants. Secondly, most Chinese scholars only study the SMEs' borrowing behaviors at the individual level, seldom conducting in-depth researches from the angle of interactions within the relationship network. Therefore, in order to overcome these weaknesses, this research aims to analyze the economic behaviors of SMEs' private borrowing behaviors from the angle of micro-Bayesian game under the network relationship.

2.3 Analysis of Private Capital Lenders and the Network Structure of SME's Borrowing

As one of the main bodies for SME' private borrowings, capital lenders seldom make their game decisions solely by themselves. No one on the nodes of the social relation network can escape from the influences of people around. They will all be influenced by others to a certain degree and thus constantly revise their original judgments. This can be clearly illustrated through the following structure of interpersonal relationship network.

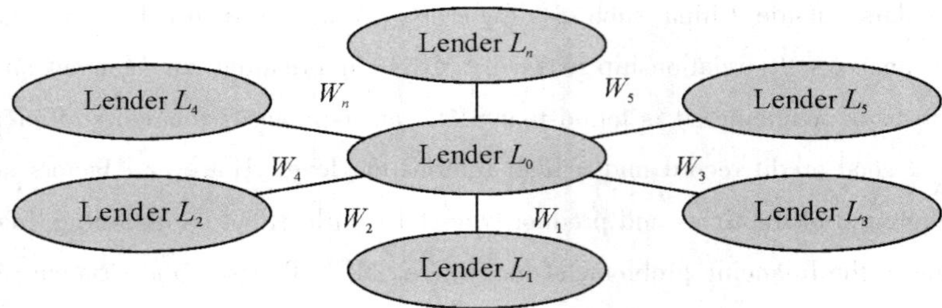

Fig. 2-1 Social Relationship Network of SME's Private Borrowing

Model assumptions:

(1) SME *A* has a prior default probability P_0, and it's known by all people.

(2) Lender L_0 will consult other people (acquaintances, friends, relatives and so on) about the possible risks before lending the money, and he or she will be affected by other people including L_1, L_2,... L_n and thus further revise his or her prior judgment.

(3) Assume that participants L_1, L_2,... L_n are independent from each other, and evidences they get about enterprise *A's* default are respectively E_1, E_2, $\cdots E_n$. Take LS_1 as L_1's judgment of SME *A*'s default intensity based on evidence E_1, and $LS_1 = P(E_1/L_0)/P(E_1/-L_0)$. Here, the bigger LS_1 is, the stronger the evidence is

in supporting the conclusion of contract breach; On the contrary, the smaller LS_1 is, the weaker the evidence will be. Moreover, assume that LN_1 is enterprise *A*'s default intensity when evidence E_1 is invalid. Similar are (LS_2, LN_2),… (LS_n, LN_n).

So when a natural person L_0 consults L_1, L_1 will tell L_0 his or her judgment based on evidence E_1, then we can calculate the LS_1 according to $LS_1 = P(E_1/L_0)/P(E_1/-L_0)$. Then, L_0's prior probability P_0 will be revised in accordance with LS_1. Thus, lender L_0's posterior probability can be obtained through subjective Bayesian formula:

$$P_1 = P(L_0/E_1) = LS_1 \cdot P_0/[(LS_1 - 1)P_0 + 1] \quad (2.1)$$

Similarly, when a natural person *A* continues to consult L_2, his or her prior probability P_0 will also be revised, so we can again obtain the posterior probability as:

$$P_2 = P(L_0/E_2) = LS_2 \cdot P_0/[(LS_2 - 1)P_0 + 1] \quad (2.2)$$

Similarly, When he or she consults L_n, his or her posterior probability is:

$$P_n = P(L_0/E_n) = LS_n \cdot P_0/[(LS_n - 1)P_0 + 1] \quad (2.3)$$

If the credit weight of E_1, E_2, $\cdots E_n$ in L_0's social relationship network is W_1, W_2, $\cdots W_n$, then the comprehensive posterior probability can be as follows:

$$P_t = W_1 \cdot P_1 + W_2 \cdot P_2 \cdots + W_1 \cdot P_n \quad (2.4)$$

To further understand how a lender can revise his or her prior judgement through his or her social relationship network, please refer to Fig. 2-1 and Fig. 2-2:

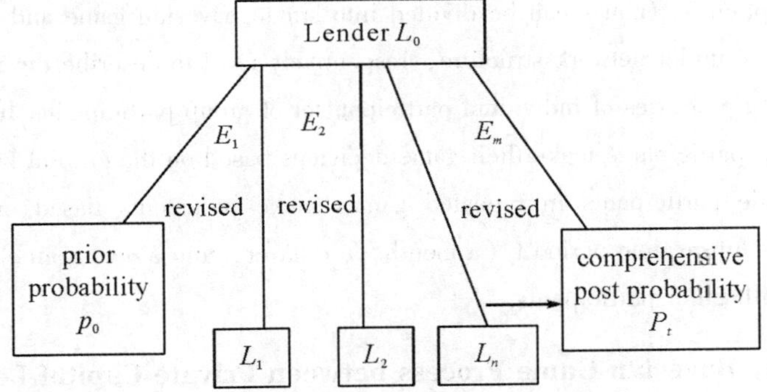

Fig. 2-2 Revision of the Prior Judgment by a Lender through His or Her Social Relationship Network

2.4 Analysis of Games between Private Capital Lenders and SME

2.4.1 Basic Assumptions of the Game Models

Private borrowing behaviors of SME are carried out among related participants. In order to well analyze the problem and simplify the model, following assumptions are made about games between SMEs and the capital lenders during the borrowing processes.

Assumption 1: Participants of Bayesian game on both sides, including both SMEs and private lenders, are completely rational. Namely, participants' economic activities are all carried out from the perspective of the maximization of their own interests. This is both a common characteristic and a common sense of all the participants.

Assumption 2: By no means can participant on one side know the strategy selection, revenue function, and the complete information of participant's characteristics of the other side. The participants can only obtain the perfect information. Their knowledge of the game process is asymmetric, and by no means can they know the game behaviors of the other side.

Assumption 3: Games can be divided into single bayesian game and multiplayer bayesian game under network structure, respectively used to describe the rational decision making processes of individual participant or of group participants. In the single static game, participants make their game decisions based on the current known information, while participants in repeated games make judgments based on the total payoff of the future time period t (a month, a quarter, and a year, etc.) under interactions with other participants.

2.4.2 Bayesian Game Process between Private Capital Lenders and SMEs

(1) If it is a one-time principal repayment contract, influence of time t on the game will be ignored, and only game players' decisions under a simple single game environment are considered.

Step one: Suppose private capital lender A has only two choices for dealing with his or her capital K_0: ①the money holder can put the money into the bank or use it for other investment, by which he or she can get the risk-free income with an average fixed interest I_0; ②the money holder can also lend the capital to SME, and thus gets the risk income with a floating interest $I_0 + I_1$.

Step two: Suppose SME invests part of the capital K_0 to real estate or other industries which can yield a ratio of return I_x, then game options of SME and the private capital lender A can be illustrated by the following game matrix in Table 2-1.

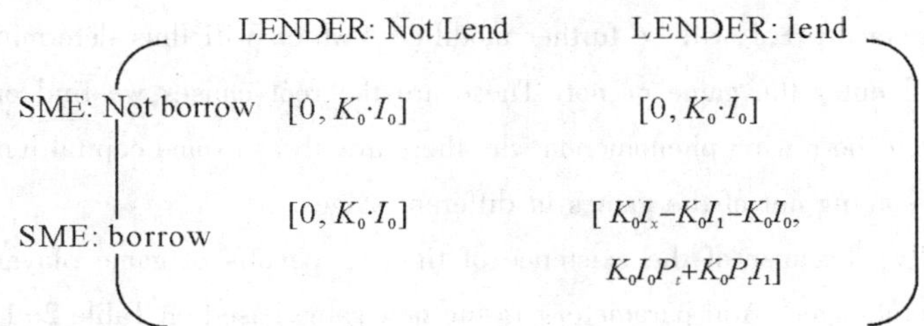

Table 2-1 Game Matrix of Private Borrowing

That is to say, SME will be quite willing to borrow money form private capital lenders as long as $K_0\ (I_x - I_1 - I_0) > 0$, namely, the future expected rate of return $I_x > I_1 + I_0$. For the lenders, as long as $K_0\ (I_0 + I_1) \cdot (1 - P_t) \geqslant K_0 \cdot I_0\ (P_t \leqslant 1 - I_0 / (I_0 + I_1))$, namely the lenders' posterior probability judgment of SME is bigger than or equal to $I_0 / (I_0 + I_1)$, they will also be very willing to lend their money. Otherwise those lenders will deposit the money in banks or involve in some other financial investments.

Nash equilibrium of the simple single static Bayesian game is $\{K_0\ (I_x - I_1 - I_0),\ K_0\ (I_0 + I_1) \cdot P_t\}$. Namely, under the equilibrium condition, SME can get a gross income $K_0\ (I_x - I_1 - I_0)$, with a rate of return $I_x - I_1 - I_0$. Private lenders can get an expected payoff of $K_0\ (I_0 + I_1) \cdot (1 - P_t)$, with a rate of return $(I_0 + I_1) \cdot (1 - P_t)$.

(2) If it is a multistage interest payment contract, considering the impact of time t on participants of both sides, payoffs and strategies of game participants on both side should be further adjusted.

First of all, because of the existence of time t, after obtaining the results of the previous games, the participants can further modify their posteriori probability judgments with the relationship network structure.

According to Fig. 2-2, if the capital lender L_n successfully gets his or her payoff during the period of time t, then he or she will modify his or her judgment of SME' default probability in stage $t+1$. For instance, if L_1's judgment of SME's default probability during the period of time t is $P(L_1)_t = 0.5$, and he or she successfully gets (doesn' t get) the payoff in t, then his or her judgment of SME' s promise (default) probability in stage $t+1$ will ascend (come down), and the result will be $P(L_1)_{t+1} > 0.5$ *or* $P(L_1)_{t+1} < 0.5$. Due to the stage change of L_n and the influences of the relationship network, the coming private capital lender A 's posterior probability judgment in stage t + 1 will be further modified, which will thus determine whether lender A will enter the game or not. These are the root causes we find out through SMEs' private borrowing phenomenon why there are always some capital lenders entering into or coming out of the games in different stages.

Secondly, because of the existence of time t, payoffs of game players on both sides will be changed. Add parameter t in the new game based on Table 2-1. Then for SME, its expected payoff in t will be:

$$G_0 = K_0 (I_x - I_1 - I_0)^t \tag{2.5}$$

As for the private capita llender, the expected payoff during the period of time t is:

$$G_t = K_0[1 + (I_0 + I_1)]^t \cdot (1 - P_{t+1}) \tag{2.6}$$

So conditions for whether the private capital lenders are willing to lend their money are changed. See followings:

$$K_0[1 + (I_0 + I_1)]^t \cdot (1 - P_{t+1}) > K_0 \cdot (1 + I_0)^t$$

so we get: $P_{t+1} < 1 - [(1 + I_0)/(1 + I_0 + I_1)$ (2.7)

So it can be seen that the bigger the value of t is, the bigger the denominator $1-[(1+I_0)/(1+I_0+I_1)]^t$ is, and the higher the requirements of the private capital lenders to the default probability P_{t+1} will be. And the value of P_{t+1} is under the influence of the game result in the previous stage, namely the influence of SME's credit level within stage t on the relationship network structure. Thus, if SMEs desire to obtain a long-term financing, they need to keep their promise in the previous stage of every stage so as to increase their credit probability $1-P_{t+1}$. And if unfortunately $P_{t+1} > 1-[(1+I_0)/(1+I_0+I_1)]^t$, some disputes like lawsuits will probably appear.

2.4.3 Case Study

A high-tech SME company borrows money from private lenders with an interest rate I_1 = 15 % per year. They agreed that the borrowing time is 5 years and the interest should be paid yearly. The enterprise has a common credit record, and its prior probability of contract default is 30% or so. *A* certain *Ms*. Zhao gets this information from her friends and relatives, and consults three persons L_1, L_2 and L_3 who are familiar with this field respectively about the relative risk. They tell Ms. Zhao their judgments of the risk (LS_1, LN_1), (LS_2, LN_2) and (LS_3, LN_3) with the values being respectively (3, 1), (1.5, 1.5), (5, 1). Then analyzing through the network structure, we can know that:

$$P_1 = LS_1 \cdot P_0/[(LS_1 - 1)P_0 + 1] = 0.375$$

$$P_2 = LS_2 \cdot P_0/[(LS_2 - 1)P_0 + 1] = 0.13$$

$$P_3 = LS_3 \cdot P_0/[(LS_3 - 1)P_0 + 1] = 0.67$$

What's more, in MS. Zhao's idea, the credit-weights of members in her social relationship network are:

$W_1 = 0.2$, $W_2 = 0.5$,. $W_3 = 0.3$

Then she can get the comprehensive posterior probability:

$$P_t = W_1 \cdot P_{t1} + W_2 \cdot P_{t2} \cdots\cdots + W_1 \cdot P_{tn} = 0.375 \times 0.2 + 0.13 \times 0.5 + 0.67 \times 0.3 = 0.341.$$

In one case, if it is a single game with a one-time principal repayment contract, then the annual risk-free interest rate in the bank (5 years) $I_0 = 7\%$. And through calculation: $I_0/(I_0+I_1) = 0.07/0.22 = 0.32$, MS. Zhao can know that $P_t = 0.341$

According to the related formula, as $P_t < 1 - I_0/(I_0 + I_1)$, Ms. Zhao will lend the money to SME.

As for SME, only when the rate of return $I_x - I_1 - I_0 > 0$ will it borrow the money. Say, $I_x > 22\%$.

In the other case, if it is a repeated game with a multi-stage interest payment contract, then Ms. Zhao should make different decisions based on the following situations:

If the enterprise doesn' t pay on schedule the interest in the first year, then she can only accept the contract when $P_{t+1} < 1 - [(1+I_0)/(1+I_0+I_1)]^t$, while when $P_{t+1} > 1 - [(1+I_0)/(1+I_0+I_1)]^t$, there may appear a contract breaching or a legal dispute.

As shown in Fig. 4, if $F(t) = 1 - [(1+I_0)/(1+I_0+I_1)]^t$, $F(t)$ will gradually approach to 1 with the increase of time t. At the same time, as shown in Fig. 2-4, with the increase of time t the value of P_{t+1} gradually approaches to 0. Then the intersection point of the two curves is just the critical point of the decision. When the capital lender faces the situation appearing on the left of the intersection point, then $P_{t+1}>1-[(1+I_0)/(1+I_0+I_1)]^t$, and thus it is very dangerous to lend the money. On the contrary, when the capital lender faces the situation appearing on the right of the intersection point, $P_{t+1}>1-[(1+I_0)/(1+I_0+I_1)]^t$, indicates that it is safe to lend the money.

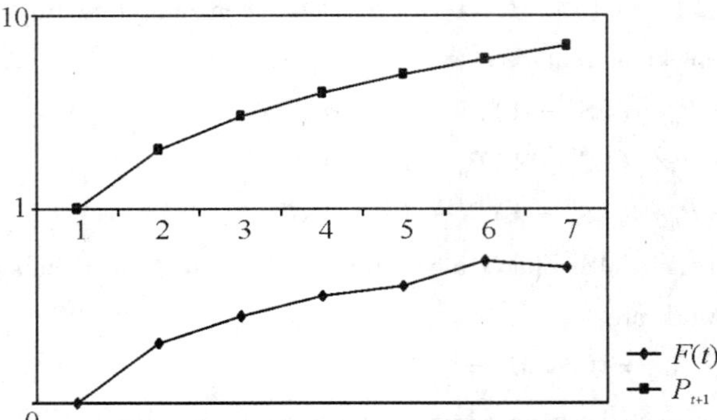

Fig. 2-3 Dynamic Changes in Repeated Game

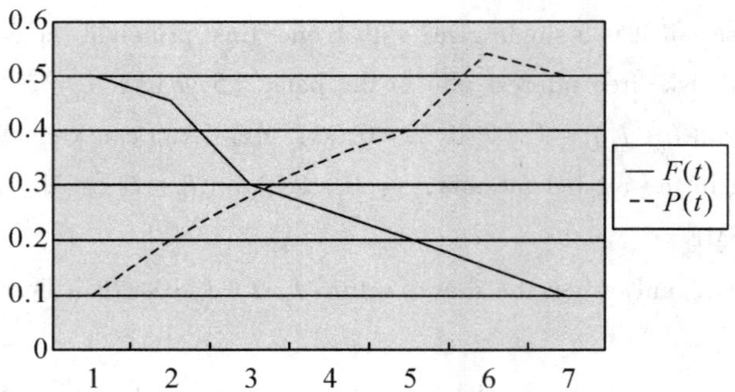

Fig. 2-4 Dynamic Equilibrium of Repeated Game

2.5 Countermeasures and Suggestions

Through the above analysis it is suggested that we make improvements from the following aspects so as to solve the problems such as information asymmetry, high risks in private borrowing as well as the high cost and less access of SME financing:

Firstly, the government should broaden the financing channels for SME, setting up more loan banks and more loan guarantee agencies suitable for SME's financing. The reliance of SME on formal credit channels can make most of the SME' private borrowing behaviors shunt or disappear. What's more, these formal financing channels can also make the mutual credit evaluations of the two sides more scientific, credit risk probability P_t much smaller and the default cost lower.

Secondly, set up more third party risk assessment organizations to professionally assess the credit risks of SME's private borrowing. Participants' assessments of LS_1, LN_1 will often be affected by their own subjectivity, which will aggravate participants' tendency of underestimating or overestimating the risks. However, the third party service institutions can just overcome this shortcoming. Professional information investigators and the information service network in the third party service institutions can offer great help in accurately grasping information including the management mode, growth, performance, and the repayment capability of a SME, so the risk of the borrowing will be decreased and the efficiency will be improved. And at the same time, it will also help to avoid the "moral hazard" and "lemon market" phenomena in the SME's private borrowing process to some extent.

Thirdly, the government should further strengthen its supervision on SME' private borrowing behaviors, so as to avoid fraud cases. The government should issue a series of laws and regulations after full discussion to regulate the private borrowing market and make clear the differences and dividing line between legal and illegal capital as well as legal loaning and illegal usury. Moreover, a special private lending supervision team dedicated to regulation of the lending behaviors should be set up by the government, so as to supervise the money lender, SME, as well as the third party service organizations together.

2.6 Conclusions

To sum up, numerous participants and aspects are involved in SME's private borrowing process. And no participant in this process can act without being affected by the complex network. Say, all the rational decisions are made under the influence of various factors. Therefore, to straighten out and standardize SME's private borrowing behaviors, the first thing to be done is to analyze the rational choices and the decision-making behaviors of the players from the microscopic viewpoint. We should grasp the nature of things, and at the same time improve the credit level of SME and guarantee the legitimate rights and interests of both parties. Only by these can we effectively regulate and guide SME's borrowing behaviors to achieve a long-term healthy development.

3 模式创新与风险控制论（一）：基于系统动力学对中小企业闭环供应链金融的动态仿真研究

3.1 引言

中小企业（SME）是我国经济增长的最具活力的推动因素。根据亚太经合组织（APEC）的相关统计：亚太地区的中小企业在促进国家经济增长、技术创新以及国民就业方面发挥着重要的作用，中小企业的GDP贡献率超过50%，就业贡献率超过60%。这一现象在中国尤为显著，我国共有中小企业5 000多万家，企业数占总数的95%以上，每年新增财富占GDP总量的50%以上，上交税额占比超过50%，而且中小企业还为社会提供了超过80%的就业机会。但是中小企业的生存状态不容乐观，麦克米伦缺口的扩大，特别是金融危机之后以及仍在持续的欧债危机所带来的负面影响，外部环境带来的对中小企业的产品需求的下降，直接导致中小企业的现金流短缺，使得中小企业不得不依靠外源性融资来维持企业的生存。

外源性融资是指企业依靠外部资金资源来维持企业的正常运转，但是外源性融资具有风险的不确定性以及风险的难控性等特点。对于金融机构来说，如何通过供应链来管控中小企业的融资风险成为重点关注的问题，因而中小企业供应链金融（SCF）模式也就应运而生。中小企业闭环供应链（CLSC）是中小企业供应链金融的一种特殊表现形式，它是指众多的中小企业围绕着一个核心企业的一个或多个核心产品而组织在一起的产业链条，产业链条上的企业相互影响、相互制约，并形成一个往复循环的企业生态系统。中小企业闭环供应链金融（SMECLSCF）是指中小企业闭环供应链上的企业为了实现资金的流转和整个生态链条的健康发展，企业间相互提供资金来源，或是核心企业提供信用担保来帮助资金短缺的企业获得信用贷款，从而实现共同成长的模式。中小企业闭环供应链金融在现实生活中得到了较为广泛的运用，特别是深圳发展银行、平安银行等在近几年推出了一系列的中小企业供应链金融产品，为我国中小企业解决融资问题做出了积极的努力。

中小企业闭环供应链金融是一个新生事物，所以不能只依靠传统的路径来分析和判断它的风险损益，中小企业闭环供应链金融应该拥有一套自己独特的风险评估以及风险控制的方法。本书在借鉴前人研究成果的基础上，通过系统动力学理论来分析与仿真实验，并提出适合中小企业闭环供应链金融的优化解决方案。

3.2 文献综述

国内外对中小企业闭环供应链金融的研究甚少，他们主要是从上一级属概念“中小企业供应链金融”方面进行的研究，主要有以下几种视角和观点：

从中小企业供应链金融模式角度进行的研究：闫俊宏和许祥秦（2007）、陈李宏和彭芳春（2008）、余剑梅（2011）等研究了中小企业供应链金融的应收款、预付款和存货的应收账款融资模式、保兑仓融资模式以及动产质押融资模式。彭柳洁（2008）、胡跃飞和黄少卿（2009）等针对中小企业供应链金融的需求进行金融产品创新和融资方案设计，在供应链上寻找多个参与者或者利益相关者，建立一种特殊的机制，来共同分担中小企业供应链金融的风险。赵亚娟、杨喜孙、刘心报（2009）等提出了中小企业利用供应链上的核心企业（CE）进行融资的模式。Stephens，Ken（2009）及 Zipkin P（2009）等针对中小企业供应链金融中的质押融资操作模式提出了可实施的质量控制方法。David A. Wuttke，Constantin Blome，Michael Henke（2013）等通过调查研究表明：中小企业供应链上的企业采用装运发货前“pre-shipment”融资模式优于“post-shipment”融资模式。

从中小企业供应链金融风险评价模型角度进行的研究：张浩（2008）、汪守国和徐莉（2009）等分析了中小企业供应链金融存在的风险，并采用层次分析法（AHP）构建了一个基于供应链金融的中小企业信用评级模型。熊熊、马佳（2009）等提出了供应链金融模式下的主成分分析（PCA）与 Logistic 回归分析两者结合的信用风险评价方法。时广静（2008）、弯红地（2008）等通过对金融供应链上的参与人的利益相关性研究，提出了应收账款融资模式的道德风险模型（MHM）。王琪（2010）等建立了基于决策树（DMT）的供应链金融模式的信用风险评估体系。周学农（2010）、何宜庆和郭婷婷（2010）、徐岩和胡斌及钱任（2011）、乔晓宇（2011）、李雯靓（2012）等运用博弈论（Game theory）为供应链金融的三种融资模式——应收账款融资模式、预付账款融资模式和存货融资模式以及中小企业贷款联盟（SMELA）分别建立了信用风险博弈模型。Tsung-Kang Chen，Hsien-Hsing Liao（2013）等建立了牛鞭效应（Chain bullwhip effect）模型来解释供应链金融企业之间风险的传递感染性。

从金融机构控制中小企业供应链金融风险的角度进行的研究：杨晏忠（2007）、田雷和刘文笑（2011）等在对商业银行供应链金融面临的风险和表现形式进行分析的基础上，提出了一些中小企业供应链金融风险控制的具体方法。周纯敏（2009）、仉瑄和李海鹏（2011）等认为商业银行要实现中小企业供应链金融的信用风险最小化的目标，需要建立应急处理机制（TETM），加强现金流控制和结构授信安排，并跟踪评价核心企业的经营情况。Brass R（2009）等认为通过加强供应链上下游企业之间的联系可以降低金融机构和企业的融资风险。Chang Hwan Lee，Byong-Duk Rhee（2011）等证明了通过企业间的协调以及商业信用的建立，中小企业供应链金融的金融风险控制效果优于金融机构面向单个企业的金融风险控制效果。

国内外学者对于中小企业供应链金融的研究不少，并得到了许多令学界瞩目的理论成果。但是这些研究还具有一些瑕疵：一是很少有学者做中小企业闭环供应链金融的研究，二是研究的体系缺乏系统性。一些学者试图通过对某一方面的研究来解决“麦克米伦缺口”问题，却忽视了对中小企业供应链金融的系统性分析（SA）和全局最优研究。本书将从中小企业闭环供应链出发，以系统论的观点去说明金融资源优化配置的方法与路径。

3.3 模型的建立与仿真分析

系统动力学（System Dynamics，SD）是系统科学的一个分支学科，它以系统的信息反馈控制为研究对象。系统动力学是由美国 MIT 的研究人员 Jay W. Forrester教授在 20 世纪中叶创立的，经过几十年的发展，系统动力学被广泛地应用于经济、管理、交通、城建、环境、生物、医学、制造、生态等多个领域。系统动力学多与其他科学如控制论、信息论、系统论、突变理论、耗散理论等结合在一起进行系统的稳定性分析、灵敏度分析、参数估计、最优化分析、类属结构分析等。

系统动力学把系统看成是多重信息反馈系统，通过研究人员对系统的深入分析，把系统分解成不同的因素集合，然后将不同的因素联系起来建立起因果关系反馈图，并通过 Vensim 软件建立系统流程图（包括 Dynamo 方程的建立与输入），最后对现实的系统结构进行仿真实验，以找出较优的系统结构。系统动力学仿真模型建立的步骤如下（图 3-1）：

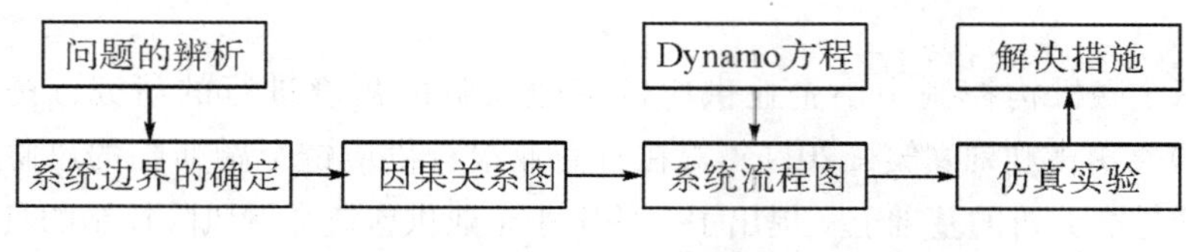

图 3-1　系统动力学仿真模型建立的步骤

3.3.1　问题的辨析

传统的中小企业供应链管理模式是基于信息流与物流的集成系统，譬如 VMI（Vendor Managed Inventory）管理系统、JMI（Jointly Managed Inventory）管理系统、CPFR（Collaborative Planning Forecasting and Replenishment）管理系统等，但是这些集成系统中没有包含资金流的因素，资金流往往独立于中小企业供应链之外。从帕累托最优的角度来看，整个供应链系统并没有实现资源的充分利用。因而，如何将中小企业供应链系统与融资系统两者有机地结合起来，使得整体系统的金融资源优化配置，实现系统的帕累托最优结果，是中小企业亟待解决的难题之一。本书基于系统动力学，从闭环供应链系统动态仿真的角度提供了一种解决此问题的关键技术与方法。

3.3.2　系统边界的确定

在中小企业闭环供应链金融系统集成中，只选取闭环供应链的核心企业、上游企业、下游企业、金融机构作为考察对象，而且主要考虑中小企业闭环供应链中的资金系统，一般不重点关注生产系统、订货系统以及物流服务系统等。

3.3.3　因果关系图

下游企业销售产品后，除去销售费用，可以按照一定的回款率获得回款资金。下游企业的资金主要用于下游企业的各种成本支出和向上游的核心企业按照一定的回款率回款；这时，如果下游企业的现金流断流，资金盈余为负数，那么下游企业可以利用商业银行的授信额度通过贷款来注入资金。

核心企业获得下游企业的回款后，同样将回款资金主要用于核心游企业的各种成本支出和向上游的企业按照一定的回款率回款，同时形成核心企业的资金盈亏。如果核心企业的盈亏情况为负数，则将通过商业银行的授信额度补充资金。核心企业与上、下游企业的不同之处在于核心企业往往在商业银行可以获得更多的授信额度。

由于是闭环供应链，上游企业出售商品给核心企业获得款项后，会将一部分资金用于购买闭环上下游企业的回收产品，还有一部分资金将用于企业留存，形成上游企业的资金盈余，其他部分资金将用于企业的各种成本支出。同样，当上游企业的资金链断裂时，它可以按照商业银行的授信额度获得部分资金的注入。

通过对中小企业闭环供应链系统的分析，我们可以用 Vensim 软件在计算机上描述出各因素之间的结构和因果关系图，如图 3-2 所示。

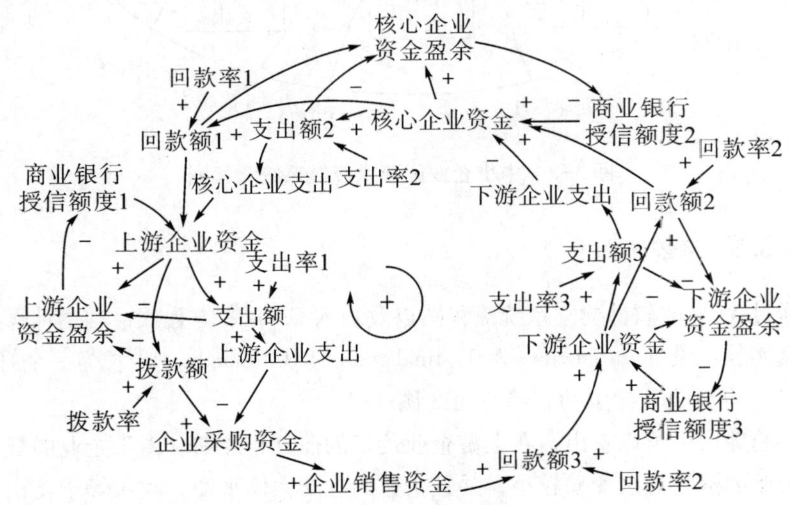

图 3-2 中小企业闭环供应链（SMECLSC）系统因果图

3.3.4 系统流程图

在上述因果关系图的基础上，按照 Vensim 软件系统流程图的建模规则：首先，确定中小企业闭环供应链的水平变量，它包括上游企业资金、下游企业资金、核心企业资金、企业销售资金、企业采购资金五个水平变量；其次，确定速率变量，它包括拨付额、支付额 1、支付额 2、支付额 3、回款额 1、回款额 2、回款额 3 这七个速率变量，以及相对应的拨付率、支付率 1、支付率 2、支付率 3、回款率 1、回款率 2、回款率 3 这七个辅助变量；此外，流图中还包括与水平变量和速率变量相对应的上游企业盈余、核心企业盈余、下游企业盈余、商业银行授信额度 1、商业银行授信额度 2、商业银行授信额度 3 这六个辅助变量。通过 Vensim 软件构建出的系统流程图如图 3-3 所示。

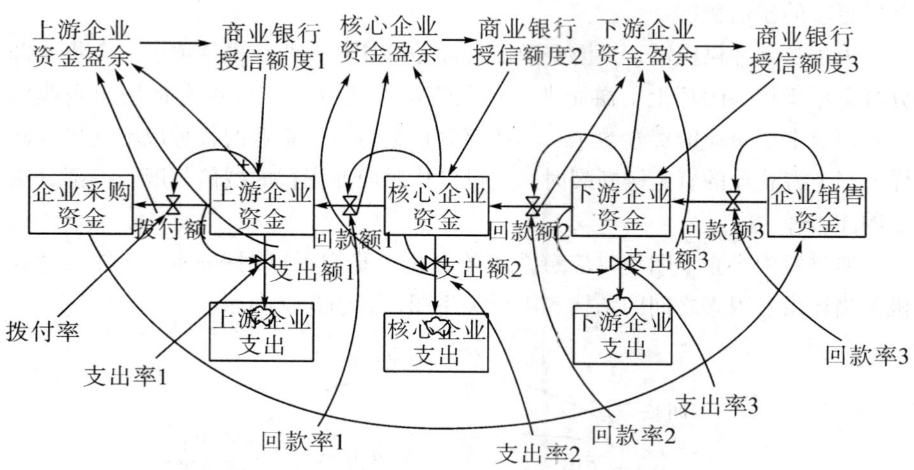

图 3-3　中小企业闭环供应链系统流程图

3.3.5　系统仿真

通过 Vensim 软件建立系统流程图以及输入 Dynamo 方程式，利用计算机进行仿真实验：设置 initial time 为 0，final time 为 100 months，步长为一个月。

（1）上游企业盈余动态趋势图（图 3-4）。

从趋势图中可以看出，在上游企业运行的前五年左右，由于企业的规模较小，企业的资金盈余变动较小，并且企业的收支大体平衡，收入等于支出，企业基本没有盈余。但在上游企业运作五年后，随着经营规模的扩大，上游企业资金盈余的波动幅度开始增加，出现频繁震荡的趋势，这时企业经营常常会出现收入小于开支或者收入大于开支的情形。当上游企业资金盈余为负数时，意味着企业处于亏损状态，即使它耗尽自己的商业银行授信额度，现金流也存在不足，所以这时候就需要从核心企业那里借入商业银行的授信额度，以增加上游企业资金的流动性，避免资金链条断裂。

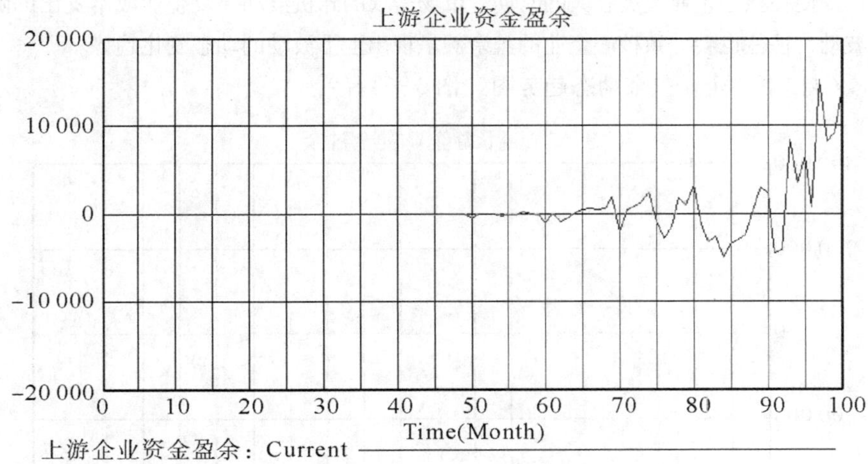

图 3-4　上游企业盈余动态趋势图

（2）核心企业盈余动态趋势图（图 3-5）。

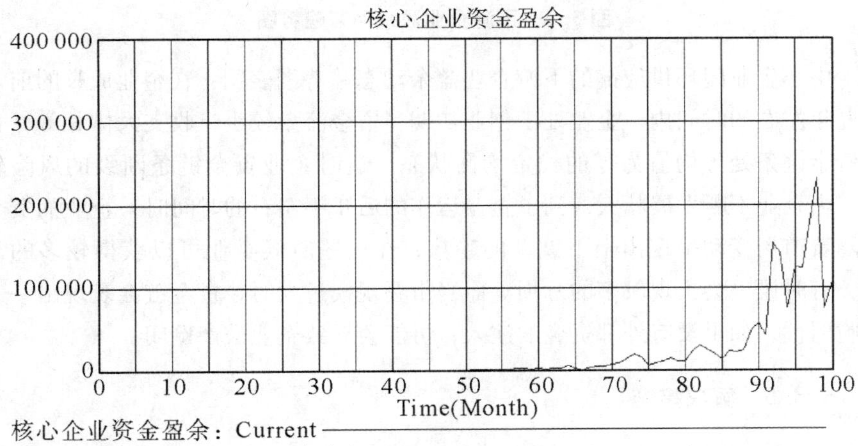

图 3-5　核心企业盈余动态趋势图

从核心企业盈余动态趋势图中可以看出，核心企业利用在中小企业闭环供应链中的核心地位，能够长时间获得更多的资金盈余，形成企业的经营利润。核心企业与上游企业一样，在企业经营的前期阶段，由于受到经营规模的影响，并不能从市场中获取超额利润，而是处于收支平衡状态，收入等于支出。只有到了核心企业经营的后期，随着中小企业产业链的升级以及企业的成长，才可以保证企业获得越来越多的资金盈余，这时候收入大于开支，并形成资金的累积。同时，我们可以观察到，即使在核心企业发展壮大的时期，市场需求的随机波动以及企业成本支出的随机波动，往往也会导致核心企业的盈余额呈现出上下波动的动态变化趋势。

（3）下游企业盈余动态趋势图（图3-6）。

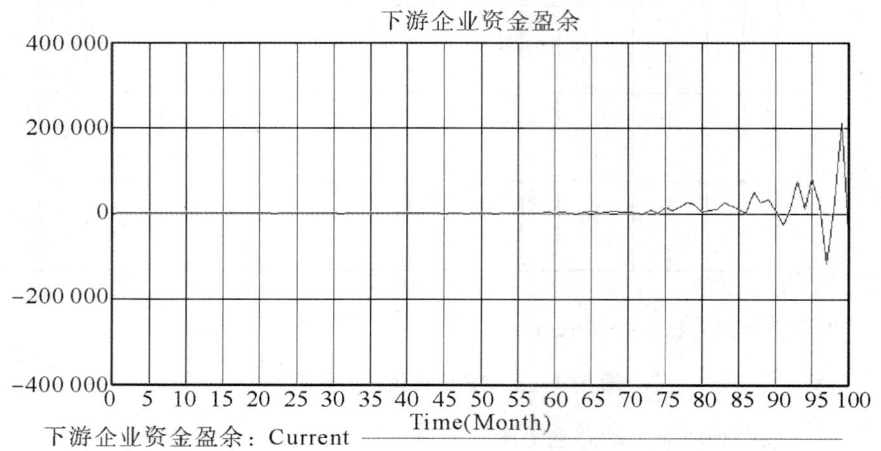

图3-6 下游企业盈余动态趋势图

中小企业闭环供应链的下游企业盈余动态趋势图表明：在企业成长的前六至七年左右的时间内，企业处于创业初期，资金流量较小，收支大体相等，企业资金链条处于均值为零的稳定均衡状态，这时企业资金链条断裂的风险较小。当企业不断发展壮大，到了企业运作的后4年左右的时间时，企业的资金链随着市场变动呈现出上下波动的趋势，在一些时候企业可以获得较多的盈利，有时候也会出现较多的亏损。而当市场规模过大时，资金链会表现出一定的脆弱性，如果没有外部资金的注入，可能会导致企业破产倒闭。

3.3.6 解决措施

通过对中小企业闭环供应链的动态仿真分析发现，核心企业与上下游企业的资金盈余动态趋势并不完全一致，当上下游中小企业处于亏损或者资金匮乏的时候，核心企业可能会有较多的闲余资金，特别是在企业发展的中后期阶段，市场风险加剧的情况下，往往可以看到这样的非同步均衡的波动趋势。中小企业闭环供应链节点上的企业相互之间是利益共同体，上下游企业的亏损或者破产可能会直接影响核心企业的生产运作，因而需要对整条供应链进行金融资源系统优化。中小企业闭环供应链金融（SMECLSCF）系统可以通过整合资源来促进闭环供应链上的企业合作共赢发挥其独特的优势：当核心企业有资金盈余的时候，可以将盈余资金以及商业银行的授信额度按照一定的协议条件调配给中下游企业，帮助闭环供应链上的中下游企业克服短期的资金困难，保持中小企业闭环供应链系统各节点企业的正常运作。按照中小企业闭环供应链金融系统的构建思路，我们对中小企业闭环供应链系统流程图增加了企业间的共享机制：一是核心企业盈余资金的共享机制；二是商业银行授信额度的授信机制。增补修正后的中小企业闭环供应链金融系统因果图，如图 3-7 所示。

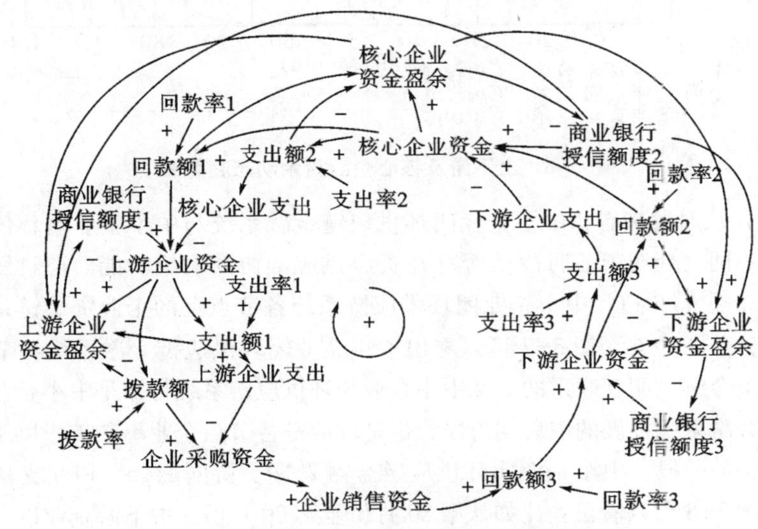

图 3-7　中小企业闭环供应链金融系统因果图

在中小企业闭环供应链金融系统因果图的基础之上构建系统流程图（由于篇幅限制省略），并在系统 Dynamo 方程所有的初始变量以及其他参数与中小企业闭环供应链系统保持一致的基础上进行仿真实验，我们可以得到以下的动态仿真结果，如图 3-8 所示。

通过对中小企业闭环供应链金融系统的上下游及核心企业盈余动态趋势图的分析，我们至少可以看出以下两种资金链系统优化的结果：

（1）从时点来看，中小企业闭环供应链金融系统改善了节点上个别企业的严重资金短缺的情况，核心企业扮演了“救生员”的角色。即使供应链金融系统上下游企业在某些时点还会出现资金短缺，但是相对于中小企业闭环供应链的波动图（参考图 3-4 和图 3-6）来说，资金的短缺量下降了数倍左右：譬如下游企业在图 3-6 中的波动曲线的谷底出现了 10 万元左右的资金短缺，但是经过系统优化，建立中小企业闭环供应链金融系统后，下游企业在图 3-8 中的波动曲线的谷底极值出现的资金短缺少于 2 万元。

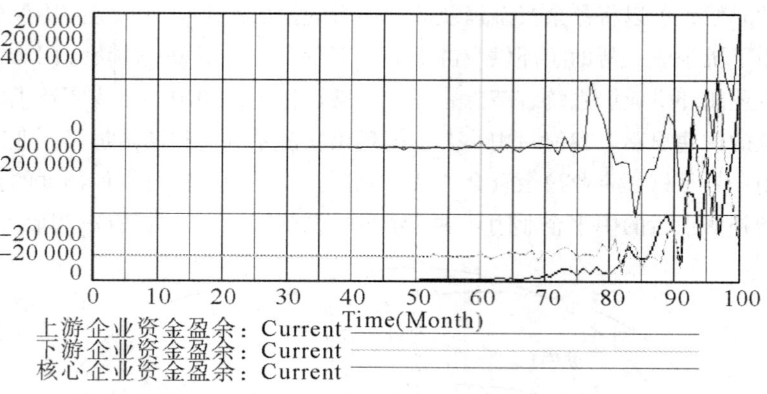

图 3-8 上下游及核心企业盈余动态趋势图

（2）从时段来看，中小企业闭环供应链金融系统与中小企业闭环供应链系统的不同之处在于各时段是否存在资金供应链协同响应功能。通过图 3-1 至图 3-5 我们知道，中小企业闭环供应链系统各节点上的企业资金链是相互独立的；从图 3-6 至图 3-7 可以看出中小企业闭环供应链金融系统各节点上企业的资金链是相互联系的。在中小企业闭环供应链系统特别是中小企业闭环供应链金融系统发展的中后期阶段，也是供应链各节点企业不断扩张以及市场风险加剧的阶段，中小企业闭环供应链金融发挥了协同配合、相互支持的作用。从图 3-8 可以看出：比如从第 80 月份至第 90 月份，中下游企业以及核心企业的资金链表现出相似的波形，即系统具有较强的协同响应功能。

3.4 总结

中小企业闭环供应链金融系统与传统的中小企业融资系统具有明显的不同。传统企业的融资主要是依靠单个企业的实力和信用度，而中小企业闭环供应链金融模式则延伸了产业链，将产业链的各个节点企业有机地联系起来，属于“群岛岛链”现象。传统的中小企业融资系统由于受“孤岛”效应的影响，企业资金链表现出一定的脆弱性，而中小企业闭环供应链金融系统的“群岛”效应则使得企业资金链更为刚性。通过对中小企业闭环供应链金融系统和中小企业闭环供应链系统进行仿真对比分析研究，找出了中小企业闭环供应链金融合作的集群优势，提出了创新的融资模式，进而减小了“麦克米伦缺口”，有助于推动中小企业闭环供应链各节点上的企业健康发展。

3 Model Innovation and Theory of Risk Control (Ⅰ): Dynamic Simulationof Small and Medium-sized Enterprise Closed-Loop Supply Chain Finance Based on System Dynamics

3.1 Introduction

Small and medium-sized enterprise is one of the most vigorous drivers of economic growth in China. According to APEC statistics: small and medium-sized enterprises (SMEs) in the Asia-Pacific region are playing an increasingly important role in economic growth, technology innovation and increasing employment opportunities (with their contribution rate in gross domestic products (GDP) exceeding 60% and in employment over 50% respectively). And this fact is especially true in China, where there are more than 5 000 SMEs, accounting for more than 95% of the country's total. In China, SMEs have created more than 60% of the newly-increased social wealth, paid over 50% of the total taxes, and brought 80% or more of the new job opportunities. Nevertheless, the survival conditions of these SMEs are not correspondingly optimistic: expanding Macmillan gap, especially the lasting fallout of the European debt crisis.... All these deteriorating external environment factors result in a declining product demand, which leads directly to their cash shortages and thus their reliance on the external financing.

External financing, namely enterprises' reliance on external financial resources to support their normal operations, is often quite risky because of its uncertainty and uncontrollability. Thus, for financial institutions, how to manage and control the financing risks of SMEs through the supply chain has become a hot issue, and the SME supply chain finance (SCF) model has correspondingly emerged. SME closed-loop supply chain (CLSC) is a special form of SMESCF. It refers to the business chain in which numerous SMEs revolve around a core enterprise's one or more core products. And as these enterprises can all exert influences on and interact with the others, they in fact form a circulatory eco-system. SMECLSCF, on the other hand, is the mode in which enterprises on the SMECLSC mutually fund each other, or the core enterprises provide guarantees to help the cash-strapped companies in obtaining credit, so as to achieve the healthy development of the entire ecological chain system. Recently, SMECLSCF has been widely applied in people's real life. Say, in China, Shenzhen Development Bank and Ping An Bank have both launched a series of SMECLSCF products, which have made positive efforts in helping the Chinese SMEs to solve their financing problems.

SMECLSCF is a relatively new concept, so we should not depend only on traditional methods to analyze its risks or advantages. In other words, it should have its unique risk assessment and control methods. Therefore, based on previous studies home and abroad, and combined with system dynamics as well as the simulation experiments, the study proposes the optimized solution for SMECLSCF.

3.2 Literature Review

According to the author's investigation, till now there are few researches on SMECLSCF in the world and they are primarily done from the perspective of the genus concept "SMESCF". The related perspectives and viewpoints are mainly as follows:

The perspective of SMESCF modes: Yan Junhong, Xu Xiangqin (2007); Chen Lihong, Peng Fangchun (2008); Yu Jianmei (2011) and others do a series of researches on the three financing modes, namely financing with receivables, prepayments or inventories accounts receivable, financing with confirming storage and financing with chattel mortgage in SMESCF. Targeting at needs of the SMESCF, Peng Liujie (2008); Hu Yuefei, Huang Shaoqing (2009) devote themselves to financial product innovation and financing scheme design, looking for multiple participants or stakeholders in the supply chain who can establish a special mechanism to jointly share the SMESCF risks. Zhao Yajuan, Yang Xisun, Liu Xinbao (2009) proposes the mode in which the SMEs depend on the core enterprise of the supply chain to finance. Stephens, Ken (2009) and Zipkin P (2009), etc. put forward a feasible quality control method for the operational mode of mortgage financing in the supply chain finance of SMEs. And investigations made by David A. Wuttke, Constantin Blome, Michael Henke (2013) indicates that it is better for the SMESC enterprises to adopt a "pre-shipment" financing mode rather than using the "post-shipment" funding mode.

The perspectives of SMESCF risk assessment models: Zhang Hao (2008); Wang Shouguo, Xu Li (2009) analyze the SMESCF risks and construct a SME credit rating model based on the supply chain finance by using analytic hierarchy process (AHP) method. Xiong Xiong, Ma Jia (2009) presents a credit risk evaluation method under the supply chain finance mode which combines the principal component analysis (PCA) and the Logistic regression analysis. By studying the participants' interrelation of benefit on the financial supply chain, Shi Guangjing (2008) and Wan Hongdi (2008) propose a moral hazard model (MHM) for the receivables financing mode. Wang Qi (2010) sets up a credit risk evaluation system of the supply chain finance mode based on the decision-making tree (DMT). By using the game theory, Zhou Xuenong (2010); He Yiqing, Guo Tingting (2010); Xu Yan, Hu Bin, Qian Ren (2011); Qiao Xiaoyu (2011); Li Wenliang (2012), et al. establish credit risk game models for the three supply chain financing modes—receivables financing mode, prepayments financing mode, inventories accounts receivable financing mode and the SME Credit Union (SMELA) respectively. Tsung-Kang Chen, Hsien-Hsing Liao (2013) establishes the chain bullwhip effect model to explain the risk infection phenomenon among SCF enterprises.

The perspective of financial institutions' control over the SMESCF risks: Based on the analysis of the risks faced by the commercial banks SCF and their forms, Yang Yanzhong (2007); Tian Lei, Liu Wenxiao (2011) et al. present some specific control methods for the SMESCF risks. Zhou Chunmin (2009); Zhang Xuan, Li Haipeng (2011) et al. believe that if commercial banks want to minimize SMESCF credit risks, they must set up emergency response mechanisms (TETM), intensify their cash flow control and structural credit arrangement, as well as trace and evaluate the operation conditions of the core enterprises. Brass R (2009) reckons that financing risks of financial institutions and enterprises can be reduced by the intensified business links between the upstream and downstream enterprises in the supply chain. Chang Hwan Lee, Byong-Duk Rhee (2011) demonstrates that through coordination and the establishment of commercial credit, the financial risk control effects of SMESCF will be better than that of the financial institutions to the individual company.

As mentioned above, there are lots of researches on SMESCF, of which many attain marvelous success. But there are still some flaws: First, few study SMECLSCF. Second, the studies are not quite systematic. Some concentrate on a certain aspect in an attempt to solve the "Macmillan gap", but ignore the systematic analysis (SA) and the overall optimization study of SMESCF. As a result, the study, starting from the SMECLSC and guided by the theory of system dynamics, illustrates ways of optimizing the allocation of financial resources.

3.3 Modeling and Simulation Analysis

As a branch of systems science, system dynamics (SD) is mainly about the control of the system feed-backs. Founded by MIT researcher Jay W. Forrester in the middle of the 20th century and after decades of development, SD is now widely applied in the fields of economics, management, transport, city construction, environment, biology, medicine, manufacturing, ecology and so on. Combined with other sciences like cybernetics, information theory, systems theory, catastrophe theory as well as the dissipate theory, it is also playing a more important role in system stability analysis, sensitivity analysis, parameter estimation, optimization analysis, and class structure analysis, etc.

SD takes all systems as multiple information feedback systems. In SD, firstly, the system, after being analyzed in-depth, will be broken into many different factor sets which will then be linked together to set up a causal relationship feedback figure. After that, the Vensim software will be used to establish a system flow chart (including establishment and input of the Dynamo equation). Finally, through simulation of the real system structure, the most satisfactory system structure will be chosen. The steps for establishing a SD simulation model are as follows (Fig. 3-1).

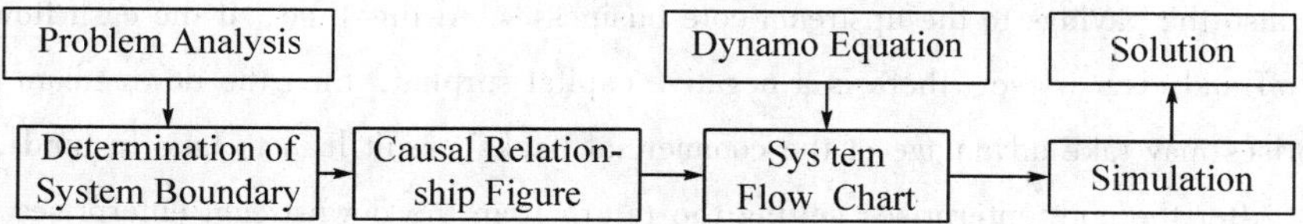

Fig. 3-1 the Steps for Establishing a SD Simulation Model

3.3.1 Problem Analysis

Traditional management modes of SME supply chain (SC), with VMI (Vendor Managed Inventory) management system, JMI (Jointly Managed Inventory) management system and CPFR (Collaborative Planning Forecasting and Replenishment) as examples, usually adopt the integration system of information flow and logistics. Nevertheless, this kind of system has not fully taken into consideration the factor of capital flow. Say, capital flow is often excluded by the SMESC. That means, from the perspective of Pareto optimal, resources in the supply chain systems as a whole have not been fully utilized . Therefore, SMEs must try their best to slove the urgent problem of how to organically combine the SMESC system and the financing system so as to realize the optimized allocation of the financial resources in the system and achieve the Pareto optimal results. Thus, with the help of SD theory, the study aims to provide a key technique and method to solve this problem from the perspective of dynamic simulation of the CLSC system.

3.3.2 Determination of the System Boundary

In the SMECLSCF integration system, select only the CLSC core enterprises, the upstream and downstream enterprises, as well as financial institutions as the target for investigation. And the focus is mainly on the SMECLSC capital systems. Generally speaking, little attention will be paid to the production systems, order systems and the logistics service systems.

3.3.3 Cause and Effect Figure

After the sales of their products, and with the sales cost excluded, the downstream enterprises can get a certain amount of return according to a certain rate, which will be thereafter used for making up various costs of the downstream enterprise and also the payings to the upstream core businesses. At this time, if the cash flow is cut off and even worse, there is a negative capital surplus, then the downstream enterprises may take advantage of the commercial banks' credit loan to take in funds.

After the core enterprises getting the return from the downstream enterprises according to a certain rate, they will also use the money to make up various costs of their own and by turn, pay the upper stream businesses and thus form the fund surplus or shortage. And if the core business faces a negative profit, they may also take advantage of the commercial banks' credit loan to inject funds. Differences between core enterprises and the upstream and downstream enterprises lie in the fact that the former can get more loans from the commercial banks than the latter.

As CLSC it is, after the upstream enterprises sell their products to the core business and get the funds, they will use part of the money to buy the recycling products from their downstream ones, with another part saved (it may become upstream capital surplus), and the rest for paying various costs. Similarly, when capital chain of the upstream enterprise ruptures, they can also take advantage of the commercial banks' credit loan to input funds.

Through the analysis of the SMECLSC system, the structure and the cause and effect figure of the factors can be described on the computer with the Vensim software as Fig. 3-2.

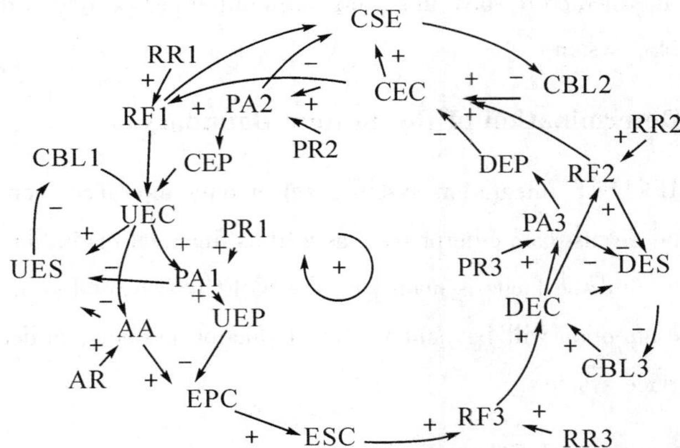

Fig. 3-2 Cause and Effect Figure of SMECLSC System

Note: simplified parameter terms in the figures.

EPC (enterprises purchase capital)

UEC (upstream enterprises capital)

CEC (core enterprises capital)

DEC (downstream enterprises capital)

ESC (enterprises sales capital)

UEP (upstream enterprises payout)

CEP (core enterprises payout)

DEP (downstream enterprises payout)

UES (upstream enterprises surplus)

CES (core enterprises surplus)

DES (downstream enterprises surplus)

CBL (commercial banks credit line)

RF (return fund)

RR (return rate)

PA (payment amount)

PR (payout rate)

AA (allocated amount)

AR (allocated rate)

3.3.4 System Flow Chart

Based on the above cause and effect figure and in accordance with the rules in Vensim for building a system flowchart: Firstly, determine the five level variables of SMECLSC including upstream enterprise capital, downstream enterprise capital, core enterprise capital, enterprise sales capital, and enterprise purchase capital; Secondly, determine seven rate variables including allocated amount, payment amount 1, payment amount 2, payment amount 3, return fund 1, return fund 2, and return fund 3; as well as the seven auxiliary variables corresponding to these rate variables including allocated rate, payout rate 1, payout rate 2, payout rate 3, return rate 1, return rate 2, and return rate 3. Besides, the flow chart also includes six other auxiliary variables in correspondence to the above-mentioned level variables and rate variables, namely upstream enterprise surplus, core enterprise surplus, downstream enterprise surplus, commercial bank credit line 1, commercial bank credit line 2, and commercial bank credit line 3. Following is the system flow figure constructed with Vensim (Fig. 3-3).

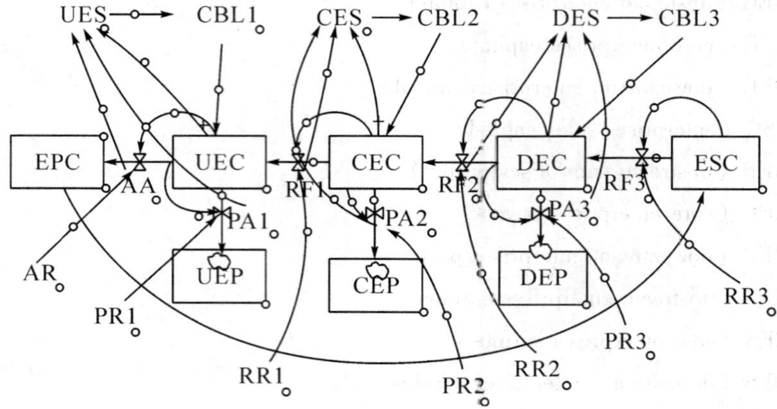

Fig. 3-3 Flow Chart of SMECLSC System

3.3.5 System Simulation

Set up the system flow chart and input the dynamo equation with Vensim and then use the computer to carry out the simulation experiment:

Setting: initial time = 0, final time = 100 months, step = 1month

(1) Dynamic Trend Figure of Upstream Enterprise Surplus (Fig. 3-4).

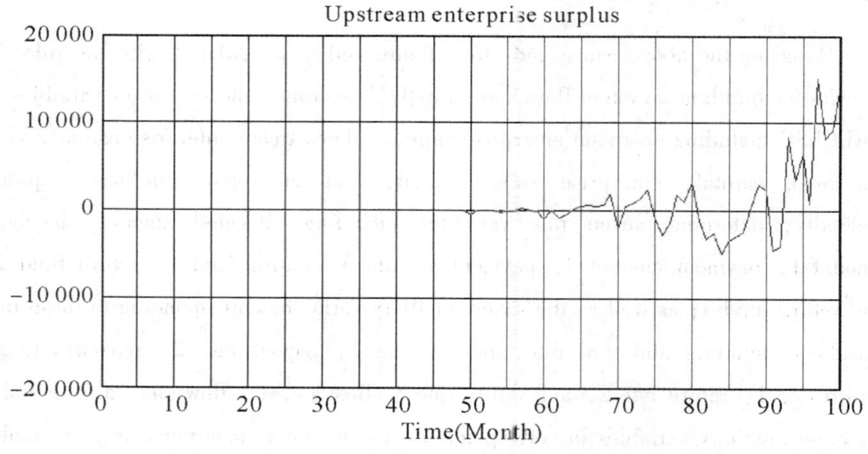

Fig. 3-4 Dynamic Trend Chart of Upstream Enterprise Surplus

Just asit is showed in the above trend chart, in the first 5 operation years of the upstream enterprise, owing to its small size, there are only small changes in its capital surplus. And generally speaking, its income and expense are balanced, namely the enterprise has basically no surplus. But after five operation years, with the expansion of its business, its capital surplus starts to swing violently and frequently (with sometimes income > expenditure, and sometimes the income < expenditure). And when the enterprise capital surplus becomes negative, which means that the enterprise is actually in loss, it will sometimes happen that even if the enterprise runs out of its own commercial bank credit line, its cash flow is still far from enough. At this time, to avoid capital chain rupture and to increase capital liquidity, the upper-stream enterprise may need to borrow from the core enterprise a certain degree of commercial bank credit line.

(2) Dynamic Trend Chart of Core Enterprise Surplus (Fig. 3-5).

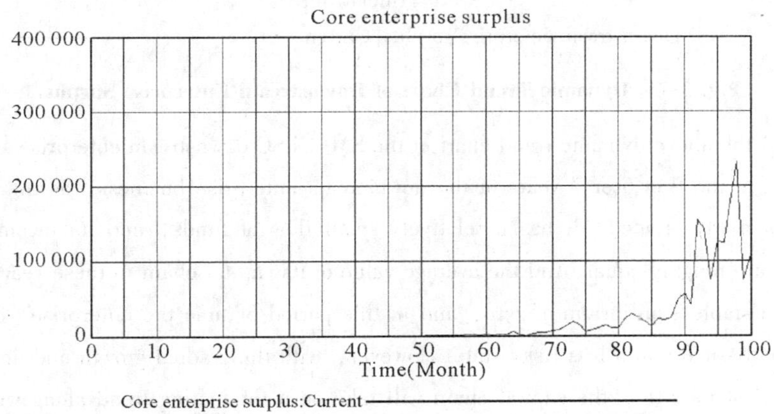

Fig. 3-5 Dynamic Trend Chart of Core Enterprise Surplus

As can be seen from the above figure, by taking advantage of its centrality in SMECLSC, core enterprise can long obtain more capital surplus and thereafter change it into profit. And just like the upstream ones, due to its comparatively small scale, the core enterprise in early stage cannot gain excessive profit from the market. Say, its income is generally equal to its payout. But in later stage of its operation, with the upgrading SME industry chain and the business growth, more capital surplus is ensured, and it appears that revenue> expenditure (the capital begins to accumulate). Meanwhile, it can also be found that even at the expansion time, the random fluctuations in market demand and changes of the private enterprises' cost payout can also lead to the dynamic fluctuations of the core enterprise surplus.

(3) Dynamic Trend Chart of Downstream Enterprise Surplus (Fig. 3-6).

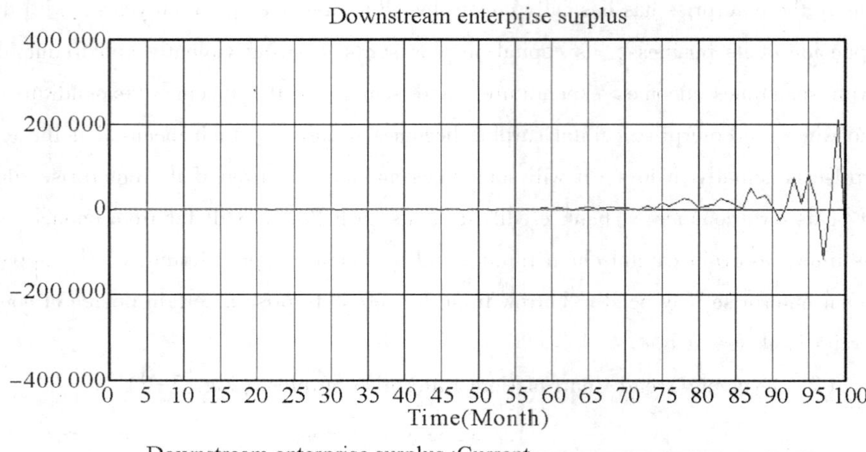

Fig. 3-6 **Dynamic Trend Chart of Downstream Enterprise Surplus**

As the above dynamic trend chart of the SMECLSC downstream enterprise surplus shows, in the first 6 or 7 years of the downstream enterprise business, as the enterprise is newly created, it has a relatively small flow of funds, and its income and payout are roughly equal. And the average value of its capital chain in these years is usually a stable equilibrium of zero, and in this period of time the enterprise's capital chain is basically at a less risky state. However, with the gradual growth and development, 4 years after, the capital chain will take on a fluctuating trend along with the market changes (There are times when companies make more money and sometimes face more losses). However, when the size of the market is too large, the financial chain will become somewhat vulnerable, and if there is no external capital injection at this point, bankruptcy will likely appear.

3.3.6 Solutions

Through dynamic simulation of the SMECLSC, it is known that the dynamic trend of the capital surplus in core enterprise is not completely consistent with that in the downstream and upstream ones. While the downstream and upstream enterprises are in lack of funds or at a loss, the core enterprise may still have certain capital surplus. Especially in the middle and the late stage of enterprise development, with the intensified market risk, this non-synchronization equilibrium fluctuation trend will be frequently caught sight of. However, as the enterprises on the SMECLSC are actually an interest community, the losses or bankruptcy of the upstream and downstream companies may have a direct impact on operation of the core ones. Therefore, at this point, it becomes necessary to optimize all the financial resources in the whole supply chain. Instead, SMECLSCF system can put its special advantages into full play by integrating resources and promoting cooperation and mutual benefits among all CLSC members: When the core enterprise has a certain capital surplus, it can lend the surplus and its extra commercial bank credit line to middlestream and downstream enterprises according to a certain agreement, so as to help the latter overcome the short-term financial obstacles and ensure the normal operation of all the node enterprises in the SMECLSC system. In accordance with the construction principles of the SMECLSCF system, the sharing mechanism among enterprises is added to the SMECLSC system flow chart, namely sharing mechanism of the core enterprise surplus capital and sharing mechanism of the commercial bank's credit line. The cause and effect figure of the amended SMECLSCF system is illustrated in Fig. 3-7.

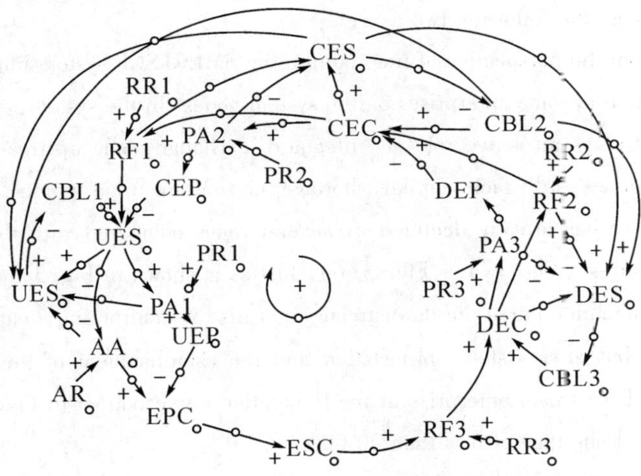

Fig. 3-7 Cause and Effect Figure of SMECLSCF System

Build system flow chart based on the above cause and effect figure of SMECLSCF system (omitted due to space restrictions) and carry out the simulation test with all the original variables and other parameters in the dynamo equations being consistent with those in the SMECLSC system. Then, the following dynamic simulation results as shown in Fig. 3-8 are obtained.

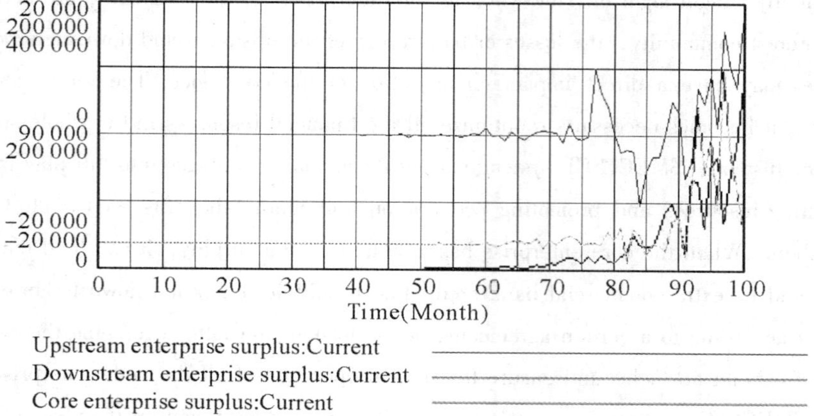

Fig. 3-8 **Dynamic Trend Flow Chart of the Upstream, Downstream and Core Enterprises**

By analyzing the dynamic trend flow chart of the upstream, downstream and core enterprises in the SMECLSCF system, we can see that the capital chain has been optimized in at least the following two aspects:

(1) From the perspective of time point, the SMECLSCF system improves the financial situation of some enterprises on the system nodes. In the system, the core business actually plays an active role of "lifeguard". Though some upstream and downstream enterprises still face capital shortage on certain time points, the capital shortage volume has already declined by several times compared with the SMECLSC fluctuation figures (Fig. 3-4 ~ Fig. 3-6). Just as is shown in Fig. 3-6, at the bottom of the fluctuation curve the downstream enterprise is confronting a capital shortage of 100 000, but after system optimization and the establishment of the SMECLSCF system, the downstream enterprise at the fluctuation curve bottom in Fig. 3-8 is only facing a capital shortage of less than 20 000.

(2) From the viewpoint of time period, the difference between SMECLSCF system and SMECLSC system mainly lies in the point whether or not the system has a capital collaborative response function during different time periods. While the enterprise capital chains on different SMECLSC nodes are all mutually independent (as it is shown in Fig. 3-1 ~ Fig. 3-5), but SMECLSCF nodes are all mutually interconnected (as it is shown in Fig. 3-6 ~ Fig. 3-7). The later development stages of

SMECLSC systems, especially of the SMECLSCF system is in fact the businesses expansion and market risk increasing stages of all the nodes on the supply chain. And at this time the SMECLSCF has actually played a role of promoting the coordination and mutual supports among all the nodes. This can be seen from Fig. 3-8, for example: from the 80th to the 90th month, capital chains of the middlestream and downstream enterprises show similar wave forms with the core enterprise, which means that the system has a strong collaborative response function.

3.4 Conclusions

SMECLSCF system is different from the traditional SME financing system. While traditional business financing system relies mainly on the strength and creditworthiness of an individual enterprise which is much similar to the "isolated island", SMECLSCF mode extends the industrial chain and organically links together the enterprises on different nodes and belongs to the "islands chain". What's more, affected by the "isolated island effect", the traditional SME financing system is to some extent fragile, but the "group islands" effect of the SMECLSCF mode on the contrary makes the enterprise capital chain more rigid. Through simulation comparison of the SMECLSC and SMECLSCF systems, the study not only finds out the cooperative cluster advantages of SMECLSCF, but also puts forward an innovative financing mode, through which it helps to decrease the "Macmillan gap" and also contribute to the healthy development of the SMECLSC enterprises.

4 模式创新与风险控制论（二）：基于演化博弈及主观贝叶斯对中小企业线上保兑仓风险的仿真研究

4.1 引言

中小企业对于国民经济的健康发展十分重要，中小企业在经济生态环境中类似于自然生态环境中的“微生物”，“微生物”不断地繁衍和死亡，不断地优胜劣汰，加速了整个生态链的进化过程。“微生物”——中小企业数量众多，约占整个企业总数的99%，解决就业数目、GDP贡献率、进出口额的贡献率、企业创新的贡献率等指标都超过了大型企业，有的指标高达70%~95%。可以说，如果一个国家的中小企业发展迟缓，那么该国经济发展的活力则将欠缺或者不足。中小企业处于企业生命周期的生长发展的初期，生命力相对来说比较脆弱；根据一些相关统计资料显示，中国的中小企业平均寿命为2.5~2.8年。对于一些夕阳产业来说，中小企业的诞生或死亡应该是一个自然过程，没有必要对其进行人为干预；但是对于一些朝阳产业和一些代表未来时代发展方向的产业，比如美国硅谷的一些高新产业，中国中关村的一些产业，在中小企业生命周期的初期阶段，就需要人为地进行“营养”“血液”的补给，以避免大规模地造成营养不良或者死亡。

首先，中小企业融资是其不断获取营养的活动，但是众所周知，由于中小企业缺乏信用记录、信贷抵押品、完整可信的财务报表等，它们很难从银行获得所需的贷款；其次，中小企业信贷的特点与大企业信贷的特点也不一样，主要表现为信贷放款时间急、信贷规模小、信贷频率高、信贷时间周期短等，银行一般的信贷产品很难满足中小企业的需求。线上供应链金融是伴随着国际互联网的发展以及供应链的发展应运而生的一种创新型的融资模式，线上供应链金融融合了互联网以及供应链两者之间的优点，具有信息共享、信息传递快、信息系统兼容等特点，能有效地解决传统融资模式的诸多难题。线上供应链金融产品与传统金融产品不同，线上供应链金融产品具有审核时间快、放贷时间快、还款时间快、信贷周期短、信贷金额小等特点，正好能适应中小企业发展的融资需求。在我国众多的商业银行中，大部分银行开展了或者准备开展线上供应链金融业务，譬如建设银行的“速贷通”、交通银行的“蕴通供应链”、中国银行的“融货达”、浦发银行的“浦发创富”、华夏银行“融资共赢链”、光大银行的“金色链”“阳光供应链”、中信银行的“银贸通”、民生银行的“贸易金融”、兴业银行的“金芝麻”等。

保兑仓业务属于供应链金融业务中的一种类型。“保兑仓”顾名思义是由“担保”“承兑”“仓库”三部分有机组成：“担保”义务是由核心企业（制造商）和物流仓库来共同履行，当下游企业（分销商）不能完全履行信贷合同义务时，将由核心企业（制造商）来履行回购物流仓库货物的义务；“承兑”是指商业银行为供应链上的核心企业开出远期承兑汇票，并届时履行承兑义务；“仓库”是连接核心企业（制造商）、下游企业（经销商）、商业银行三者之间的中转平台，核心企业（制造商）与下游企业（经销商）之间的物流速度与量的大小需要通过物流仓库来控制，商业银行也通过物流仓库出具的仓单来监管质押货物的数量，以控制信贷规模和风险的大小。“保兑仓”产品蕴含着商业银行、核心企业、中小下游企业等几个参与主体之间的博弈行为，并且这种博弈行为随着时间的推移而不断地进行演化。在博弈的演化进程中，风险是持续动态变化的，而商业银行选择什么样的方法来动态评估和控制“保兑仓”产品的风险是本书研究的主要内容之一。

传统的保兑仓业务是一种线下业务，随着计算机应用的普及以及国际互联网的快速发展，保兑仓业务很快转变成了线上与线下相结合的一种模式，近年来，在平安银行等商业银行体系中逐步发展成以线上为主的一种业务模式。

4.2 国内外文献研究综述

4.2.1 国外学者对线上供应链金融及保兑仓的研究

Faulkner，Charles（2006）指出创新技术能够降低供应链金融的成本。Brass R（2009）认为线上供应链金融可以降低风险和融资成本。Zipkin P

（2009）以及 Stephens，Ken（2009）都对线上供应链金融的不同的抵押物、质押物的质量标准以及评价方法、原则等做了详细的研究。Basu P，Nair S（2012）认为供应链金融有助于企业及时地获得现金流。Wuttke D，Blome C，Foerst K，Henke M（2013）通过对欧洲六家企业的经验证据的研究，指出买家与卖家相互交织构建的供应链金融体系能够提高资金的利用率和降低资金成本。More D，Basu P（2013）利用层次分析法，以印度公司为样本，研究了供应链金融面临的挑战，包括比如知识的缺乏、互联网等工具使用的培训机会少，以及自动化处理流程不完善等。

4.2.2 国内学者对于供应链金融之保兑仓的研究主要基于以下两个视角

（1）从保兑仓的现实意义与操作模式的角度研究。白少布、刘洪（2009）指出如果保兑仓业务的参与人要实现共赢，企业的信用水平和参与人的努力程度则不可或缺。甄莹、芦玮（2009）说明了钢铁企业保兑仓业务如何实现的问题。史丽媛、叶蜀君（2010）研究了物流企业运用仓单质押和保兑仓模式实现增值的过程。通过仓单质押模式和保兑仓模式，分析了第三方物流企业、银行、融资企业如何在实际运作过程中实现自身的增值。房艳蕾、张义刚（2010）指出了中小企业开展保兑仓业务的意义。王超（2011）从保兑仓的角度研究了供应链金融模式的运作机理、供应链整体的收益以及银行的运作决策，并从不同参与主体的角度分析了发展供应链金融的意义。钟佳萌（2012）建立了零售商在约束条件下的报童模型来预测未来的最佳订货量。林强、李晓征、师杰（2014）通过对保兑仓业务各参与人的博弈分析，认为集中决策以及数量折扣能改善供应链金融参与人的收益值。

（2）从保兑仓的风险评估与控制的角度研究。王珍（2009）以太钢为例，说明了保兑仓业务如何控制其业务风险。郭胜圣（2011）以供应链金融的保兑仓业务为研究对象，在报童模型的基础上，构建了保兑仓业务的运作模型，认为供应链金融的保兑仓能够降低企业的融资风险。杜永斌（2011）提出了我国健全商业银行保兑仓业务风险控制内容体系的具体要求，并对商业银行保兑仓业务风险控制的内容体系进行了实证分析。王儒泉（2013）从实际问题出发，从银行的角度，针对每个具体问题分别提出了具有实操性的风险控制对策，如加强准入、动态监控、信用增级、完善条款、账户监管、设定退出策略等。任慧军、李智慧、方毅（2013）对保兑仓业务存在风险的各个环节进行了分析，并提出了防范风险的措施和建议。颜明、王军、张继霞、李娟（2013）采用 VAR 模型对保兑仓的回购数量、保证金数量与业务风险三者之间的关系进行了研究。吴泽莹（2014）选取保兑仓业务作为研究对象，从收益共享契约、回购担保和信用风险评价等方面进行了研究。

4.2.3 国内外研究评述

国外有不少学者研究中小企业线上供应链金融，他们主要是基于互联网创新的角度对线上供应链金融的融资成本与新技术挑战进行研究。“保兑仓”是我国商业银行为线上供应链的中小企业设计的创新型金融产品，国外学者并不十分了解“保兑仓”的运作流程与运作模式。我国学者对“保兑仓”的研究成果比较丰富，但是这些研究主要是从定性的角度来进行描述，并没有从定量的角度去探究“保兑仓”背后的运行机理，也很少有学者运用定量的手段去评价和控制“保兑仓”的连续动态风险。在前人研究成果的基础上，创新性地运用演化博弈推演均衡解以及研究解的稳定性，同时利用社会网络关系模型和主观贝叶斯风险概率测算来研究“保兑仓”产品的风险动态评估以及实现对风险的动态控制。

4.3 中小企业线上供应链金融之保兑仓演化博弈分析

4.3.1 博弈模型假设

（1）假定参与人都是理性经济人，以追求企业的利润最大化为目的。

（2）假定博弈的类型是不完全信息博弈，彼此信息不对称。

（3）假定博弈的参与人为商业银行、核心企业、下游企业、第三方物流仓库。

（4）假设在核心企业、下游企业、第三方物流仓库中以核心企业为主导，核心企业具有企业融资的决策权。

4.3.2 模型的建立

（1）保兑仓作为供应链融资的一种创新模式，正是围绕着供应链“1+N”来进行产品设计（图4-1）。

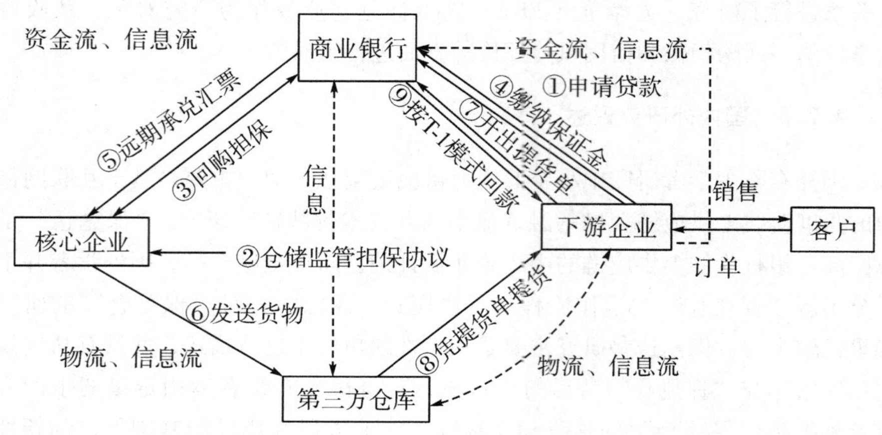

图 4-1　线上供应链金融之保兑仓应用流程图

保兑仓业务的博弈者包括商业银行、核心企业、客户、第三方仓库、下游企业。

另外，该业务还涉及现金流和信息流以及物流和信息流。

（2）线上供应链金融之保兑仓演化博弈分析。

通过对线上供应链金融之保兑仓各参与人的博弈分析，我们可以得到表 4-1的收益矩阵。

表 4-1　　线上供应链金融之保兑仓博弈收益矩阵分析

<table>
<tr><th></th><th colspan="2">商业银行（合作）P_1</th><th colspan="2">商业银行（不合作）$(1-P_1)$</th></tr>
<tr><td>核心企业（合作）P_2</td><td>$M \cdot R_1-C_1$</td><td rowspan="3">$M \cdot r-C_4$</td><td>$-C_1$</td><td rowspan="3">0</td></tr>
<tr><td>下游贷款企业（合作）P_2</td><td>$M \cdot R_2-C_2$</td><td>$-C_2$</td></tr>
<tr><td>第三方物流仓库(合作)P_2</td><td>$M \cdot R_3-C_3$</td><td>$-C_3$</td></tr>
<tr><td>核心企业（不合作）$1-P_2$</td><td rowspan="3">0</td><td rowspan="3">$-C_4$</td><td rowspan="3">0</td><td rowspan="3">0</td></tr>
<tr><td>下游贷款企业（不合作）$1-P_2$</td></tr>
<tr><td>第三方物流仓库(不合作)$1-P_2$</td></tr>
</table>

①不考虑商业银行，当供应链体系的所有企业都采取合作或者不合作策略时候，供应链上企业的期望收益为：

对于核心企业来说，收益值 $U_1=(M \cdot R_1-C_1) \cdot P_2+P_2 \cdot (-C_1)$　(4.1)

对于下游贷款企业来说，收益值 $U_2=(M\cdot R_2-C_2)\cdot P_2+P_2\cdot(-C_2)$ (4.2)

对于第三方物流企业来说，收益值 $U_3=(M\cdot R_3-C_3)\cdot P_2+P_2\cdot(-C_3)$ (4.3)

②当考虑商业银行的合作或者不合作策略，供应链企业采取合作或者不合作策略时，商业银行以 P_1 的概率采取合作策略和以 $(1-P_1)$ 采取不合作策略时，单个供应链企业的期望收益分别为：

对于核心企业来说，期望收益值为：

$$\overline{U4}=P_1\cdot(M\cdot R_1-C_1)\cdot P_2+(1-P_1)\cdot P_2\cdot(-C_1)=P_1\cdot P_2\cdot M\cdot R_1-P_2\cdot C_1 \tag{4.4}$$

对于下游贷款企业来说，期望收益值为：

$$\overline{U5}=P_1\cdot(M\cdot R_2-C_2)\cdot P_2+(1-P_1)\cdot P_2\cdot(-C_2)=P_1\cdot P_2\cdot M\cdot R_2-P_2\cdot C_2 \tag{4.5}$$

对于第三方物流企业来说，期望收益值为：

$$\overline{U6}=P_1\cdot(M\cdot R_3-C_3)\cdot P_2+(1-P_1)\cdot P_2\cdot(-C_3)=P_1\cdot P_2\cdot M\cdot R_3-P_2\cdot C_3 \tag{4.6}$$

③根据供应链企业以上的收益函数，可以写出其动态演化博弈的微分方程为：

$$F(x_1)=DP_2/D_t=P_2(U_1-\overline{U4})=P_2\cdot[P_2\cdot M\cdot R_1(1-P_1)-P_2\cdot C_1] \tag{4.7}$$

或者 $F(x_2)=P_2(U_2-\overline{U5})=P_2\cdot[P_2\cdot M\cdot R_2(1-P_1)-P_2\cdot C_2]$ (4.8)

或者 $F(x_3)=P_2(U_3-\overline{U6})=P_2\cdot[P_2\cdot M\cdot R_3(1-P_1)-P_2\cdot C_3]$ (4.9)

④当商业银行采取合作策略，供应链企业也采取合作策略时，商业银行的收益为：

$$U_7=P_1\cdot(M\cdot r-C_4)\cdot P_2 \tag{4.10}$$

当商业银行采取合作策略，供应链企业采取不合作策略时，商业银行的收益为：

$$U_8=P_1\cdot(-C_4)\cdot(1-P_2) \tag{4.11}$$

当商业银行采取不合作策略时，无论供应链企业采取什么策略，商业银行的收益为：

$$U_9=0 \tag{4.12}$$

⑤当商业银行采取合作或者不合作策略时，还需要考虑供应链上企业的合作或者不合作策略。供应链企业以 P_2 的概率采取合作策略，以（$1-P_2$）采取不合作策略时，商业银行的期望收益为：

$$\bar{U}b=U7+U8=P_1\cdot(M\cdot r-C_4)\cdot P_2+P_1\cdot(-C_4)\cdot(1-P_2)=P_1\cdot P_2\cdot M\cdot r-P_1\cdot C_4 \tag{4.13}$$

⑥根据商业银行以上的收益函数，可以写出其动态演化博弈的微分方程为：

$$F(y)=DP_1/D_t=P_1\cdot(U7-\bar{U}b)=P_1\cdot(P_1\cdot P_2\cdot M\cdot r-P_1\cdot C_4) \tag{4.14}$$

⑦众所周知，核心企业是供应链上的主导力量，具有博弈的话语权。那么如果要得到整个系统的均衡状态，需要同时满足下列方程组：

$$\begin{cases}F(y)=DP_{1/}D_t=0\\F(x_1)=DP_{2/}D_t=0\end{cases} \tag{4.15}$$

可以求得：

$(0,0)$；$(0,C_4/M\cdot r)$；$\{(1+C_1/M\cdot R_1),0\}$；$\{(1+C_1/M\cdot R_1),C_4/M\cdot r\}$ 四个点为系统的均衡点。但是四个点中有些演化博弈非稳定解，我们可以通过建立雅克比矩阵的方法来寻找演化稳定策略（ESS）均衡点：

$$J=\begin{Bmatrix}\partial F(y)/\partial P_1 & \partial F(y)/\partial P_2\\ \partial F(x)/\partial P_1 & \partial F(x)/\partial P_2\end{Bmatrix}$$

$$=\begin{Bmatrix}2P_1\cdot(P_2\cdot M\cdot r-C_4) & P_1\cdot P_1\cdot M\cdot r\\ -P_2\cdot P_2\cdot M\cdot R_1 & 2P_2\cdot M\cdot R_1(1-P_1)-2P_2\cdot C_2\end{Bmatrix}$$

要获得演化稳定策略 ESS，则需要满足 $det(J)>0$，$tr(A)<0$。

所以在（0，0）均衡点，$det(A)=0$，$tr(A)=0$，为不稳定点。

在 $(0,C_4/M\cdot r)$ 均衡点，$det(A)=0$，$tr(A)>0$，为不稳定点。

在 $\{(1-1/M\cdot R_1),0\}$ 均衡点，$det(A)=0$，$tr(A)<0$，为不稳定点。

在 $\{(1-1/M\cdot R_1),C_4/M\cdot r\}$ 均衡点，$det(A)>0$，$tr(A)<0$，为 ESS 进化稳定点。

见表 4-2 所示。

表 4-2　　　　　　　　系统动态演化 ESS 点判定表

均衡点（P_1，P_2）	DetJ	Tr	结论
$P_1=0$，$P_2=0$	0	0	不稳定解
$P_1=0$，$P_2=C_4/M\cdot r$	0	>0	不稳定解
$P_1=1-1/M\cdot R_1$，$P_2=0$	0	<0	不稳定解
$P_1=1-1/M\cdot R_1$，$P_2=C_4/M\cdot r$	>0	<0	ESS

⑧在线上供应链金融之保兑仓动态演化 ESS 均衡点判定表的基础上，我们可以做出该系统动态演化博弈图，如图 4-2 所示：

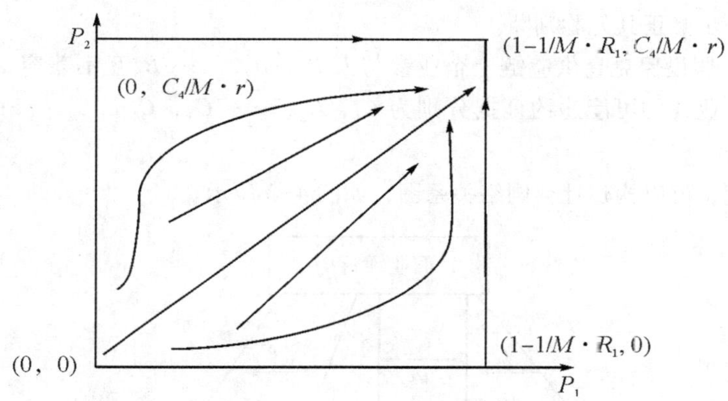

图 4-2　线上供应链金融之保兑仓动态演化博弈分析

从图 4-2 可知，存在演化博弈稳定点，即商业银行与供应链企业（以核心企业为例）向点（P_1，P_2）=（$1-1/M\cdot R_1$，$P_2=C_4/M\cdot r$）的合作概率方向稳定演化。供应链上贷款中小企业的信用风险存在时间序列动态连续性波动变化。通过演化博弈不能完全评估控制系统的实时动态风险的大小，但是商业银行在信贷过程中需要评估和控制贷款企业的实时风险，所以我们需要进一步通过社会网络贝叶斯分析来研究和掌握实时信用风险动态变化的大小情况。

4.4　社会网络下中小企业线上供应链金融之保兑仓主观贝叶斯分析

作为供应链中小企业融资的信贷方，商业银行不会单单依赖下游融资企业的财务等状况单独地做出博弈决策，而是会受到供应链上核心企业、第三方物流仓库等参与主体不同程度的影响，从而不断修正其原初的判断。可以通过中小企业的社会网络结构的主观贝叶斯模型分析来说明这一问题。

4.4.1 模型的建立与分析

模型假设：

（1）保兑中小企业 A（下游企业）的违约概率有一个先验违约概率 P_0，它对于商业银行等参与人来说是共有知识。

（2）商业银行 B_0在做出信贷之前会调查保兑中小企业 A 违约风险的大小。此后，商业银行还会受到保兑仓供应链上企业参与人 B_1，B_2，……B_N的影响，从而进一步修正其先验判断。

（3）假设保兑仓供应链上企业参与人 B_1，B_2，……B_N互不兼容，关于保兑中小企业 A 的可能违约证据分别为 C_1，C_2，……C_N，$C_1 \, U \, C_2 U \cdots\cdots U \, C_N = \Omega$。

因此，可以构建社会网络关系图，如图 4-3 所示。

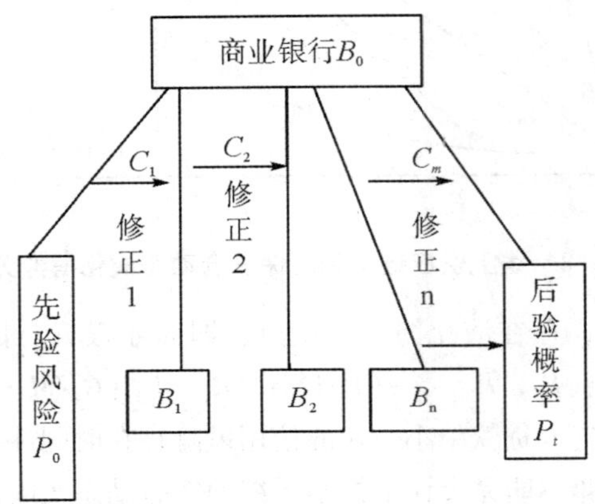

图 4-3 中小企业供应链金融之保兑仓社会网络的主观贝叶斯关系图

根据主观贝叶斯理论模型：假定 LS_1代表 B_1根据证据 C_1成立时判断保兑中小企业 A 违约的强度，LS_1越大，说明证据支持违约结论；相反，LS_1越小，证据越不支持。假定 LN_1代表证据 C_1不成立时判断保兑中小企业 A 违约的强度。同理（LS_2，LN_2），……（LSn，LNn）亦是如此。

所以，当自然人 B_0向 B_1调查信息的时候，B_1根据证据 C_1判断告知 B_0他关于（LS_1，LN_1）大小的判断。B_0根据（LS_1，LN_1）会修正先验概率 P_0的大小，根据主观贝叶斯公式可以求得出借人 B_0 的后验违约概率为：

$$P_{t1}=P\ (B_0/C_1)\ =LS_1\cdot P_0/[\ (LS_1-1)\ P_0+1]\tag{4.16}$$

当自然人 B_0 继续向 B_2 咨询的时候，也会修正先验违约概率 P_0 的大小，那么可以求得后验违约概率为：

$$P_{t2}=P\ (B_0/C_2)\ =LS_2\cdot P_{t1}/[\ (LS_2-1)\ P_{t1}+1]\tag{4.17}$$

同理，向 Bn 咨询的后验违约概率为：

$$P_{tn}=P\ (B_0/C_n)\ =LSn\cdot P_{t(n-1)}/[\ (LSn-1)\ P_{t(n-1)}+1]\tag{4.18}$$

我们也可以通过以下基于 Simulink 系统仿真实验设计的社会网络主观贝叶斯系统来进行仿真计算（图 4-4）：

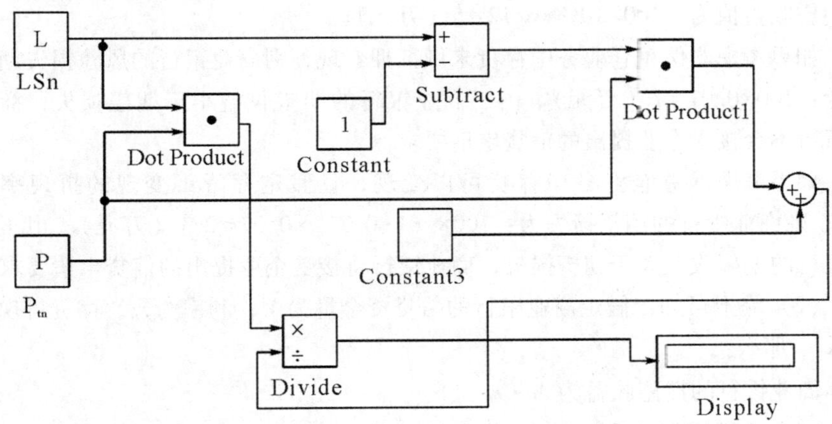

图 4-4 线上保兑仓业务社会网络主观贝叶斯仿真系统分析图

4.4.2 案例分析

供应链上某下游中小企业资金流动性紧张，该下游企业为供应链核心企业的生意长期合作伙伴，考虑到对整个供应链的影响，下游企业联合供应链核心企业以及第三方物流仓库等相关企业为其向商业银行申请保兑仓产品信贷业务。假定借款金额为 100 万元，商业银行的年利率为 10%，借款期限为 6 个月。该供应链企业信用评级较为良好，先验违约概率 P_0 为 10%。商业银行在获得供应链下游企业保兑仓产品信贷申请后，对供应链上的企业进行信用调查以及动态的信用管理，商业银行分别向上游企业 B_1、B_2、B_3 以及核心企业 B_4 和第三方物流企业 B_5 等企业进行信用调查，这些相关企业的风险违约判断（LS_1，LN_1），（LS_2，LN_2）……（LS_5，LN_5）的大小分别为（3，LN_1），（0.5，LN_2），（1，LN_3），（0.5，LN_4），（0.9，LN_5），那么通过网络结构分析及仿真运算可以得到：

$$P_{t1}=P\ (X_0/C_1)=LS_1\cdot P_0/\ [\ (LS_1-1)\ P_0+1]=0.25 \quad (4.19)$$

$$P_{t2}=P\ (X_0/C_2)=LS_2\cdot P_{t1}/\ [\ (LS_2-1)\ P_{t1}+1]=0.143 \quad (4.20)$$

$$P_{t3}=P\ (X_0/C_3)=LS_2\cdot P_{t2}/\ [\ (LS_2-1)\ P_{t2}+1]=0.143 \quad (4.21)$$

$$P_{t4}=P\ (X_0/C_4)=LS_2\cdot P_{t3}/\ [\ (LS_2-1)\ P_{t3}+1]=0.073 \quad (4.22)$$

$$P_{t5}=P\ (X_0/C5)=LS_2\cdot P_{t4}/\ [\ (LS_2-1)\ P_{t4}+1]=0.07 \quad (4.23)$$

商业银行通过对供应链上下游等相关企业进行征信调查后的后验概率为：$P_t=0.022$

（1）假定供应链下游企业的信贷时间为 6 个月，则商业银行年利率 10% 的期望收益值为：100×10%×6/12=5（万元）。

如果考虑非保兑仓业务中存货未做抵押变现，则商业银行的风险损失期望值为：100×0.07=7（万元）。由于商业银行的期望收益小于期望损失，商业银行将不会接受企业提出的信贷申请要求。

如果考虑保兑仓业务中存货可以变现，且假定存货可变现的折现率为 0.7，则商业银行的期望损失为：100×（1−0.7）×0.07=2.1（万元）。由于商业银行的期望收益大于期望损失，商业银行将接受企业提出的信贷申请要求。

（2）综上可知：假定商业银行的信贷资金量为 M，利率为 r_0，存货折现率为 R_1，那么：

商业银行的期望收益为 $M\cdot r_0$。

商业银行的期望损失为 $M\cdot P_{tn}\cdot\ (1-R_1)$。

当 $M\cdot r_0>M\cdot P_{tn}\cdot\ (1-R_1)$ 时，即 $P_{tn}<r_0/\ (1-R_1)$ 时，即商业银行愿意信贷给供应链上的中小保兑企业。

当 $M\cdot r_0<M\cdot P_{tn}\cdot\ (1-R_1)$ 时，即 $P_{tn}>r_0/\ (1-R_1)$ 时，商业银行将不愿意信贷给供应链上的中小保兑企业。

由于市场的变化，R_1 是动态变化的；商业银行实施动态信用调查，所以 P_{tn} 也是不断变化的。我们可以通过图 4-5 来分析商业银行对中小企业供应链金融之保兑仓业务的决策方法。

在 t_n 时刻，$P_{tn}=r_0/\ (1-R_1)$，这是商业银行动态决策的均衡点，如果 P_{tn} 继续向下偏离均衡点，$r_0/\ (1-R_1)$ 继续向上偏离均衡点，那么商业银行可以做出向供应链上的中小企业借出保兑仓信贷的决策（如图 4-5 所示）。如果向相反的均衡点方向偏离，则商业银行可能做出拒绝信贷要求的决策。

同时，我们也可以利用 *Simulink* 对该系统进行数值仿真研究。假定 LS=3，$P=0.1$，$r_0=0.1$。根据保兑仓质押商品特性的不同，我们可以把商品分为价值

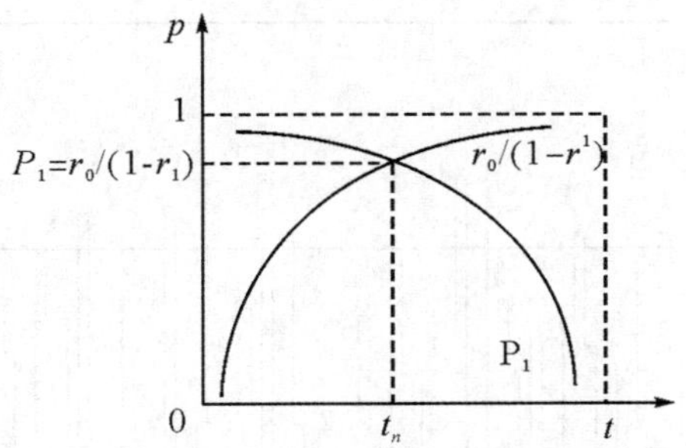

图 4-5　商业银行动态决策图

随市场随机波动的商品（如船舶、车辆、房地产等）和价值随时间发展不断递减的商品（如蔬菜、水果、时装等）。对于前者，R_1的输入函数为随机波动函数，质押价值的波动范围为（0.2~0.65）（图 4-7）；对于后者，R_1为斜坡函数，斜率为 0.09（图 4-8）。通过仿真运行可看到如图 4-6 至图 4-8 所示。

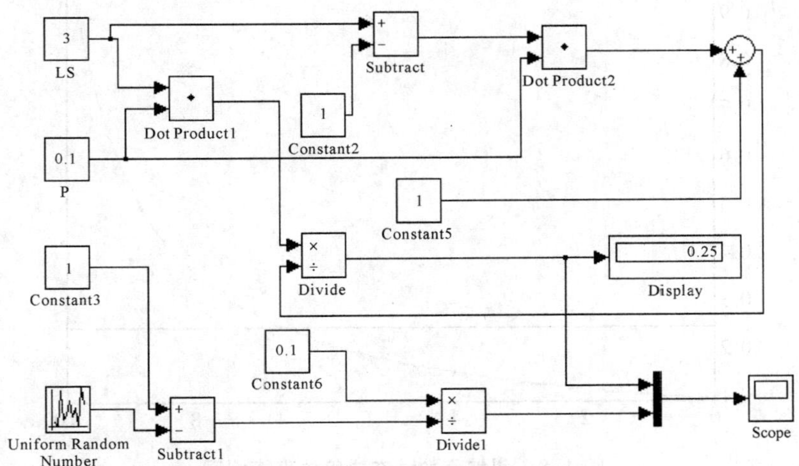

图 4-6　商业银行对保兑仓业务系统动态决策的仿真系统

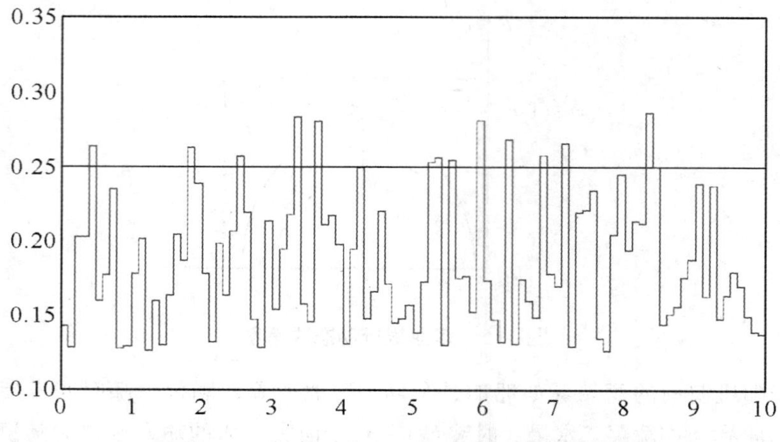

图 4-7　随机波动函数动态决策仿真模拟图

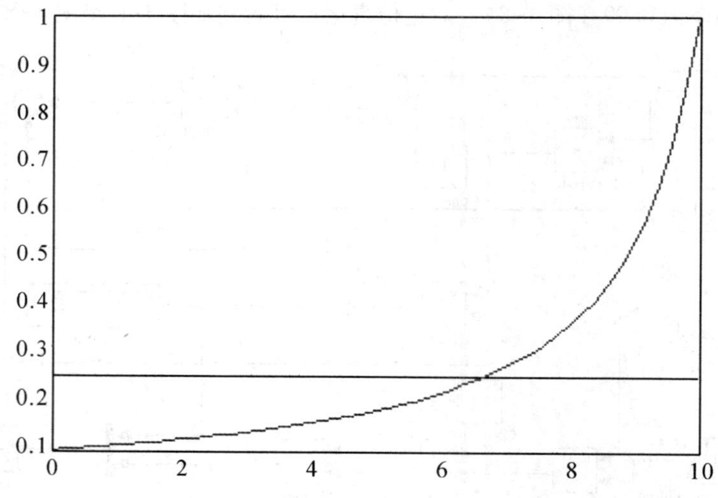

图 4-8　斜坡函数动态决策仿真模拟图

如图 4-7 和图 4-8 所示，当时间序列波动曲线位于直线下方时，商业银行对中小企业的线上供应链金融业务是安全的。一旦时间波动曲线位于直线上方，则说明信贷风险较高，商业银行应该紧缩信贷业务或者取消该中小企业保兑仓的信贷业务，从而有效地预防和控制商业银行的信贷风险。

4.5 总结

融资一直是全球中小企业乃至整个世界经济发展的瓶颈。尽管这一问题引起了世界各国的高度重视，但是至今仍未能取得十分令人满意的结果。本书从微观的角度，即从商业银行具体的融资创新产品模式——“中小企业供应链保兑仓”入手，来分析商业银行与供应链中小企业的演化博弈过程以及博弈的均衡解，并通过均衡解试图寻找演化博弈的稳定性。当系统缺乏稳定性时，则需要对“保兑仓”系统进行融资风险评估，本书采用了一种在实践业务中方便易行的评估方法——“基于社会网络模型的主观贝叶斯风险估计”，经过对模型的推演以及案例的模拟，我们认为这种方法是一种较优的动态决策方法，能够有效地解决融资实践中存在的问题。

4 Model Innovation and Theory of Risk Control (Ⅱ): Simulation Research onRisks of SME On-line Confirming Storage Business Based on Evolutionary Game Theory and Subjective Bayesian Method

4.1 Introduction

Small and medium-sized enterprises (SMEs), very much similar to the "microorganisms" in nature, is vitally important for the healthy development of national economy. These "microorganisms" continually multiply, die and compete with each other, by which they greatly speed up the evolution process of the whole ecological chain. Taking up about 99% of the total enterprises, these "microorganisms", i. e., the SMEs have made great contributions to employment, GDP, import and export, enterprise innovation, and so on. Their contribution index even surpasses that of large enterprises, some being up to 70%~95%. Safely speaking, if the development of SMEs in a country is delayed, then it will surely result in inadequate vitality of the country's economy. As is known to all, as the initial stage of enterprises' life cycle, SMEs are relatively fragile. According to related statistics, average life expectancy of SMEs in China is as short as 2.5~2.8 years. For some sunset industries, birth or death of SMEs is just a natural process, which means that there is no need for intervention on purpose; but for those sunrise industries and those which represent the future development direction of the times, like some high-tech industries in U. S. Silicon Valley and China's Zhongguancun, "nutrition" and "blood" must be injected into SMEs at their early stage so as to avoid mass malnutrition or death.

Financing is the main source for SMEs' nutrition and energy. However, it is also known to all that financing in SMEs is no easy work. Firstly, lacking good credit records, convincing guarantees, complete and credible financial reports, it is difficult for SMEs to get necessary loans from banks; secondly, SME loans are quite different from those of large enterprise for they are featured by relative urgency, small-scale, high frequency, and short cycle . Thus, the common credit products in banks can hardly meet their loan demands. On the contrary, online supply chain financing, an innovative financing mode appearing with the development of internet and supply chain, can better deal with these bottlenecks in traditional modes as they have the characteristics of better information-sharing, quick information transmission, compatible information systems, etc. Different from the traditional products, online supply chain financing is featured by a shorter audit time, shorter lending time, fast repayment, shorter credit cycle, as well as small loan amount which can better cater SMEs' demands. Currently, most commercial banks in China have already had or at least have prepared online supply chain financing products. Examples include the online supply chain financing products "Su Dai Tong (Easy Loan)" of China Construction Bank, "Yun Tong supply chain" of Bank of Communications, "Rong Tong Da" of Bank of China, "Pufa Chuang Fu" of Shanghai Pudong Development Bank, "Rong Zi Gong Ying Lian" of Hua Xia Bank, "Jin Se Lian" "Yang Guang Gong Ying Lian" of China Everbright Bank, "Yin Mao Tong" of China Citic Bank, "Mao Yi Jin Rong" of China Minsheng Banking and "Jin Zhi Ma" of China's Industrial Bank, etc.

Confirming storage is one type of such supply chain financing. As suggested by its Chinese name "Bao Dui Cang", confirming storage business includes three organic parts, namely "guarantee (保)" "acceptance (兑)" and "storage (仓)". Among them, the first part— "guarantee" will mainly be carried out by core enterprises (manufacturers) and logistic warehouse together. When downstream enterprises (distributors) fail to fulfill the contract duty, the core enterprises will shoulder the obligation of repurchasing the goods in the warehouse. The second part "acceptance" —refers to the fact that commercial banks will issue usance acceptance for core enterprises of the supply chain, and they will also be responsible for fulfilling the corresponding acceptance duty when the time comes. The third part— "storage" is the transfer platform among the core enterprises, the downstream distributors and the commercial banks. It controls the logistic speed and amount between the core enterprises (manufacturers) and the downstream distributors. It also issues warehouse receipts to help commercial banks supervise the number of mortgages, by which the commercial banks can better control the credit scale and the risks. Thus we can say that the confirming storage business is actually a game action which is continually evolving over time among the core enterprises, the downstream SMEs and the commercial banks. What's more, the risk in the evolutionary process is quite dynamic and it is always changing. Then what kind of strategies will be adopted by commercial banks for the assessment and control of the product risks? That is the very topic that will be concentrated on in this research.

One point should be noted here is that traditional confirming storage business is usually offline business. However, along with the increasing popularity of computers and internet, it quickly develops into the online and offline combined form. Recently, the online mode even turns into a dominant form in the systems of some commercial banks such as that of Ping An Banks in China, etc..

4.2 Literature Review

4.2.1 Previous Studies of Online Supply Chain Financing and Confirming Storage Business in Countries Other than China

Faulkner, Charles (2006) points out new and innovative technologies can decrease the supply chain cost. Brass R (2009) believes that online supply chain financing can lower the cost and risks of financing. Targeting at online supply chain financing, Zipkin P (2009); Stephens, Ken (2009) make detailed studies of its mortgages and their quality standards, assessment methods and assessment principles. Basu P, Nair S (2012) holds that supply chain financing can help enterprises obtain cash in time. Through an experimental study of six European enterprises, Wuttke D, Blome C, Foerst K, Henke M (2013) claims that the supply chain financing system mutually set up by the seller and the buyer can help increase the capital utilization rate and at the same time low down the capital cost. Taking an Indian company as the example and taking advantage of Analytic Hierarchy Process (AHP), More D, Basu P

(2013) studies the challenges faced by the supply chain financing, such as lacking of necessary knowledge, inadequate training in use of internet tools and imperfect automation processes, etc..

4.2.2 Previous Studies of Online Supply Chain Financing and Confirming Storage Business in China

Previous researches on confirming storage business of supply chain financing in China are mainly done from two perspectives:

(1) Significance and operation modes of confirming storage: Bai Shaobu, Liu hong (2009) points out that if the confirming storage participants want to achieve a win-win situation, a high enterprise credit level and the participants' effort are indispensable. Zhen Ying, LuWei (2009) discusses how an iron and steel enterprise can start its confirming storage business. Shi Liyuan, Ye Shujun (2010) makes research on how the logistics enterprises make use of warehouse receipt pledge and confirming storage business mode to have their own value increased. They also analyze how the third party enterprises, banks and financing companies can increase their own values in the operation process by the same means. Fang Yanlei, Zhang Yigang (2010) points out the significance of confirming storage business in SMEs From the perspective of confirming storage business, Wang Chao (2011) first studies the operation mechanism of supply chain financing model, earnings of the supply chain as a whole and the operational decisions of the banks; and then from the perspective of different participants, He analyzes the significance of developing the supply chain financing. Zhong Jiameng (2012) establishes a newsboy model for retailers under constraint conditions to help them predict the future optimal order amount. Through analysis of the game participants in the confirming storage business, Ling Qiang, Li Xiaozheng, Shi Jie (2014) states that centralized decision-making and quantity discount can improve the profit for the supply chain financing participants.

(2) Assessment and control of confirming storage risks: Taking Taiyuan Iron and Steel Co . as an example, Wang Zhen (2009) illustrates how to control the risks faced by confirming storage business. Taking confirming storage business of supply chain financing as the research object and the newsboy model as the basis, Guo Shengsheng (2011) constructs the operation model for the business and believes that it can reduce the corporate financing risk. Du Yongbin (2011) specifies the

standards for how to perfect the confirming storage risk control system and makes an empirical analysis of the system in commercial banks. Starting from some problems in actual operation of banks, Wang Ruquan (2013) puts forward some practical risk control methods, such as the access controlling, dynamic monitoring, credit enhancement, provision improvement, account supervision, exit strategy setting, etc. Ren Huijun, Li Zhihui, Fang Yi (2013) analyzes the risks in confirming storage process and also puts forward some suggestions and prevention measures for risk control. By using the VAR model, Yan Ming, Wang Jun, Zhang Jixia, Li Juan (2013) focuses on the relationship among the repurchase amount, the cash deposit amount and the business risk in confirming storage business. Again targeting at the confirming storage business, Wu Zeying (2014) makes some studies from the perspective of gains sharing contract, repurchase guarantee and credit risk evaluation and so on.

4.2.3 Comments on the Previous Studies

To sum up, researchers from countries other than China have made lots of studies of SME online supply chain financing. From the perspective of internet innovation, they mainly focus on the challenges brought by new technologies to online supply chain financing as well as its cost. Confirming storage is an innovative financing product designed by China's commercial banks for SMEs in supply chain, and its mode and operation process are rarely known by the researchers in other countries. In China, studies of confirming storage business are comparatively fruitful. However, these studies are mainly some qualitative ones. Instead, there are few researches concerning the operation mechanism, the assessment and control of its risks from the quantitative point of view. Therefore, based on the previous studies, the research aims to innovatively adopt the evolutionary game method to study the equilibrium and its stability. And at the same time, it also employs the social network model and the subjective Bayesian risk estimation method to dynamically assess and control the confirming storage risks.

4.3 Evolutionary Game Analysis of Confirming storage business in SME Online Supply Chain Financing

4.3.1 Assumptions in the Game Model

(1) Assume that participants are all rational economic persons in pursuit of profit maximization of the enterprise.

(2) Assume that the game studied here is one with incomplete information, and participants here can only obtain asymmetric information.

(3) Assume that game participants here include commercial banks, core enterprises, downstream enterprises and the third-party logistics warehouse.

(4) Assume that the core enterprise is the decisive party among the three, namely the core enterprise, the downstream enterprise and the third-party logistic warehouse, and it has the decision-making power in the enterprise financing process.

4.3.2 Establishment of the Model

(1) As an innovative mode of supply chain financing, confirming storage is designed based on the supply chain "1+N".

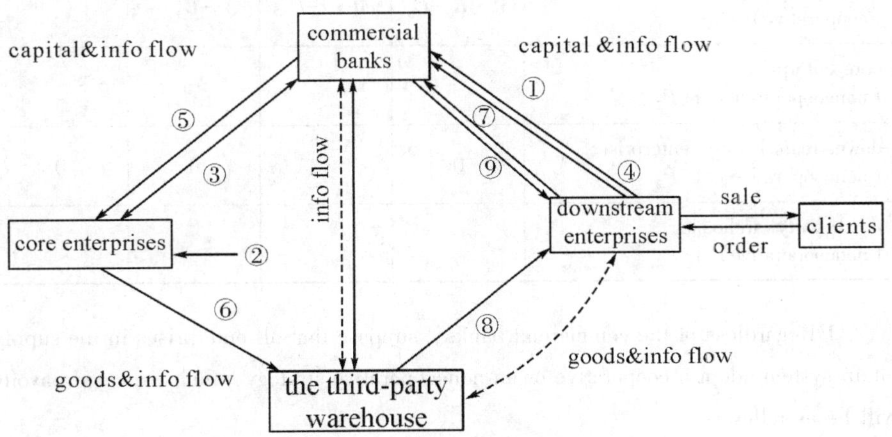

Fig. 4-1 Application Flow Chart of Confirming Storage in Online Supply Chain Financing

Notes: ① loan application; ② warehouse supervision guarantee agreement; ③repurchase guarantee; ④payment guarantee; ⑤Usance acceptance ⑥goods delivery; ⑦B/L issuing; ⑧picking up goods with B/L; ⑨returning funds by $T-1$ mode.

Game participants of confirming storage business include commercial banks, core enterprises, clients, the third-party warehouse, and the downstream enterprises.

Other factorsinvolved in this business include cash flow and information flow, logistics and information flow.

(2) Evolutionary game analysis of confirming storage business in online supply chain financing

By analyzing the game among participants of confirming storage business in online supply chain financing, the following payoff matrix can be obtained:

Table 4-1 Payoff Matrix of Confirming Storage Business in Online Supply Chain Financing

	Commercial banks (cooperative) P_1		Commercial banks (noncooperative) $(1-P_1)$	
core enterprises (cooperative) P_2	$M \cdot R_1-C_1$		$-C_1$	0
downstream borrowing enterprises (cooperative) P_2	$M \cdot R_2-C_2$	$M \cdot r-C_4$	$-C_2$	0
third-party warehouses (cooperative) P_2	$M \cdot R_3-C_3$	$M \cdot r-C_4$	$-C_3$	
core enterprises (noncooperative) $1-P_2$				
downstream loaning enterprises (noncooperative) $1-P_2$	0	$-C_4$	0	0
third-partywarehouses (noncooperative) $1-P_2$				

①Regardless of the commercial banks, suppose that all enterprises in the supply chain system adopt a cooperative or an noncooperative strategy, their expected payoffs will be as follows:

Payoff for core enterprises: $U_1 = (M \cdot R_1-C_1) \cdot P_2+P_2 \cdot (-C_1)$ (4.1)

Payoff for downstream borrowing enterprises: $U_2 = (M \cdot R_2-C_2) \cdot P_2+ P_2 \cdot (-C_2)$ (4.2)

Payoff for the third-party warehouses: $U_3 = (M \cdot R_3 - C_3) \cdot P_2 + P_2 \cdot (-C_3)$ (4.3)

②Take the cooperative or noncooperative strategy of commercial banks into consideration. When the supply chain enterprise adopt a cooperative or noncooperative strategy, and when commercial banks adopt a cooperative strategy with the probability P_1, or an noncooperative strategy with the probability $(1-P_1)$, the expected payoff for a single enterprise on the supply chain will be:

Expected payoff for the core enterprise:

$$\overline{U4} = P_1 \cdot (M \cdot R_1 - C_1) \cdot P_2 + (1-P_1) \cdot P_2 \cdot (-C_1) = P_1 \cdot P_2 \cdot M \cdot R_1 - P_2 \cdot C_1 \quad (4.4)$$

Expected payoff for the downstream loaning enterprise:

$$\overline{U5} = P_1 \cdot (M \cdot R_2 - C_2) \cdot P_2 + (1-P_1) \cdot P_2 \cdot (-C_2) = P_1 \cdot P_2 \cdot M \cdot R_2 - P_2 \cdot C_2 \quad (4.5)$$

Expected payoff for the third-party warehouse:

$$\overline{U6} = P_1 \cdot (M \cdot R_3 - C_3) \cdot P_2 + (1-P_1) \cdot P_2 \cdot (-C_3) = P_1 \cdot P_2 \cdot M \cdot R_3 - P_2 \cdot C_3 \quad (4.6)$$

③According to above payoff functions of the supply chain enterprises, the following differential equation of dynamic evolution game can be achieved:

$$F(x_1) = DP_2/D_t = P_2(U_1 - \overline{U4}) = P_2 \cdot [P_2 \cdot M \cdot R_1 (1-P_1) - P_2 \cdot C_1] \quad (4.7)$$

$$\text{or } F(x_2) = P_2(U_2 - \overline{U5}) = P_2 \cdot [P_2 \cdot M \cdot R_2 (1-P_1) - P_2 \cdot C_2] \quad (4.8)$$

$$\text{or } F(x_3) = P_2(U_3 - \overline{U6}) = P_2 \cdot [P_2 \cdot M \cdot R_3 (1-P_1) - P_2 \cdot C_3] \quad (4.9)$$

④ When both the commercial bank and supply chain enterprises adopt cooperative strategies, the payoff for commercial bank will be:

$$U_7 = P_1 \cdot (M \cdot r - C_4) \cdot P_2 \quad (4.10)$$

When the commercial bank adopts a cooperative strategy and the supply chain enterprises adopt noncooperative strategies, the payoff for the commercial bank will be:

$$U_8 = P_1 \cdot (-C_4) \cdot (1-P_2) \quad (4.11)$$

When the commercial bank adopt noncooperative strategies, then whatever strategies will the supply chain enterprises adopt, the payoff for the commercial bank will be:

$$U_9 = 0 \quad (4.12)$$

⑤When commercial banks take a cooperative or non-cooperative strategy, they also need to take the supply chain enterprises' strategies into consideration. When the supply chain enterprises take a cooperative strategy with the probability P_2, or a non-cooperation strategy with the probability $(1-P_2)$, the expected payoff for the commercial banks will be:

$$\bar{Ub} = U7 + U8 = P_1 \cdot (M \cdot r - C_4) \cdot P_2 + P_1 \cdot (-C_4) \cdot (1 - P_2) = P_1 \cdot P_2 \cdot M \cdot r - P_1 \cdot C_4 \quad (4.13)$$

⑥Based on the above payoff functions for commercial banks, the following differential equation of dynamic evolution game can be attained:

$$F(y) = DP_1/D_t = P_1 \cdot (U_7 - \bar{Ub}) = P_1 \cdot (P_1 \cdot P_2 \cdot M \cdot r - P_1 \cdot C_4) \quad (4.14)$$

⑦Just as is known to all, the core enterprise is the leading force in the supply chain which has the discourse power and right in the game. Then the following equation group must be met if one wants to get the equilibrium of the whole system:

$$F(y) = DP_{1/}D_t = 0$$
$$\mathrm{F}(\mathrm{x}_1) = \mathrm{DP}_{2/}\mathrm{D}_t = 0 \quad (4.15)$$

So four equilibrium point of the system can be attained:

$(0, 0)$; $(0, C_4/M \cdot r)$; $\{(1+C_1/M \cdot R_1), 0\}$; $\{(1+C_1/M \cdot R_1), C_4/M \cdot r\}$

However, some of these four points are instable solutions of the evolutionary game and the Jacobian matrix can be set up to find out the evolutionary stable strategy (ESS) equilibrium:

$$J = \begin{Bmatrix} \partial F(y)/\partial P_1 & \partial F(y)/\partial P_2 \\ \partial F(x)/\partial P_1 & \partial F(x)/\partial P_2 \end{Bmatrix}$$

$$= \begin{Bmatrix} 2P_1 \cdot (P_2 \cdot M \cdot r - C_4) & P_1 \cdot P_1 \cdot M \cdot r \\ -P_2 \cdot P_2 \cdot M \cdot R_1 & 2P_2 \cdot M \cdot R_1(1 - P_1) - 2P_2 \cdot C_2 \end{Bmatrix}$$

If the EES is to be found, then it should meet: $det\ (J) > 0$, $tr\ (A) < 0$.

At the equilibrium point $(0, 0)$, $det\ (A) = 0$, $tr\ (A) = 0$. Thus it is an unstable point.

At the equilibrium point $(0, C_4/M \cdot r)$, $det\ (A) = 0$, $tr\ (A) > 0$. Thus it is an unstable point.

At the equilibrium point $\{(1-1/M \cdot R_1), 0\}$, $det\ (A) = 0$, $tr\ (A) < 0$. Thus it is an unstable point.

At the equilibrium point $\{(1-1/M \cdot R_1), C_4/M \cdot r\}$, $det\ (A) > 0$,

$tr\ (A)$ <0. Thus it is the ESS point.

Table 4-2　　the Evolutionary Stable Strategy (ESS) Point

Equilibrium point (P_1, P_2)	$DetJ$	Tr	conclusion
$P_1=0,\ P_2=0$	0	0	unstable
$P_1=0,\ P_2=C_4/M \cdot r$	0	>0	unstable
$P_1=1-1/M \cdot R_1,\ P_2=0$	0	<0	unstable
$P_1=1-1/M \cdot R_1,\ P_2=C_4/M \cdot r$	>0	<0	ESS

⑧Based on the above decision table of the ESS point for the confirming storage, we can draw out the dynamic evolutionary game analysis chart of the system as indicated in the following Fig. 4-2.

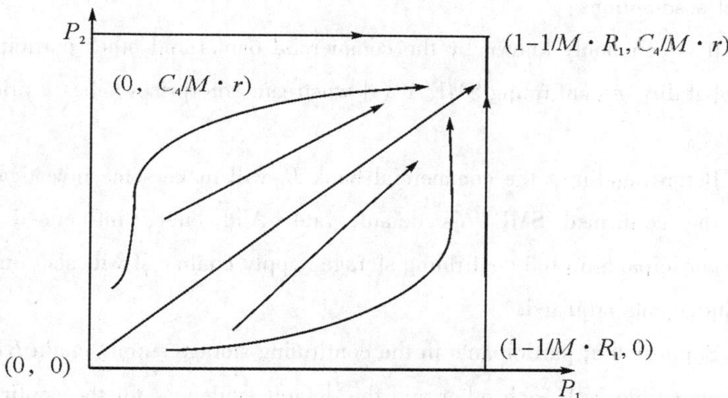

Fig. 4-2　Dynamic Evolutionary Game Analysis of Confirming Storage Business in Online Supply Chain Financing

The above game analysis chart clearly shows the ESS equilibrium point. That is to say, commercial banks and supply chain enterprises (the core enterprises, for example) steadily evolves to the direction of the cooperation probability $(P_1, P_2) = (1-1/M \cdot R_1,\ P_2=C_4/M \cdot r)$. Credit risks of loaning SMEs in the supply chain take on dynamic and continuous fluctuations along with the time changes. Thus one cannot completely assess the real-time dynamic risks of the controlling system only by the evolutionary game. However, it is just the very task of commercial banks. Thus, Bayesian analysis of social networks should be further adopted to analyze the dynamic changes of real-time credit risks.

4.4 Subjective Bayesian Analysis of Confirming Storage in SME Online Supply Chain Financing under Social Network

As the lending party for SMEs on the supply chain, commercial banks will not make their game decisions solely by judging the financial states of the downstream financing enterprises, but will also constantly adjust their judgments based on different actions of the core enterprises and the third party logistics warehouses. This can be illustrated by the subjective Bayasian game model of SME social network.

4.4.1 Establishment and Analysis of the Model

Model assumptions:

(1) It is commonly known by the commercial banks and other participants that default probability of confirming SME A (downstream enterprises) has a prior default probability P_0.

(2) Before lending, the commercial bank B_0 will make some investigations targeting at the confirmed SME A's default rate. And later, influenced by other enterprise participants in the confirming storage supply chain, it will also further have its priori judgments adjusted.

(3) Suppose that participants in the confirming storage supply chain $B1$, $B2$,... Bn are incompatible with each other and the default evidences for the confirmed SME A are C_1, C_2, ⋯, Cn, $C_1\ U\ C_2 U \cdots U\ Cn = \Omega$.

Then, a social networkfigure as below can be built:

According to the subjective Bayesian model: Assume that LS_1 is the default rate judged by B_1 for SME_A when evidence C_1 is true. Then the bigger the LS_1 is, the more likely that SME A will default, and vice versa. Assume that LN_1 stands for the default rate of SME_A when evidence C_1 is false. Similar are $(\mathrm{LS}_2, \mathrm{LN}_2)$, ⋯ $(\mathrm{LS}_n, \mathrm{LN}_n)$.

Thus, when a natural person B_0 asks B_1 for some information, B_1 will tell B_0 its judgment of $(\mathrm{LS}_1, \mathrm{LN}_1)$ based on evidence C_1. Then B_0 will adjust its prior probability P_0. According to subjective Bayesian formula, the posterior default probability of lender B_0 can be obtained as follows:

$$P_{t1} = P(B_0/C_1) = \mathrm{LS}_1 \cdot P_0/[(\mathrm{LS}_1 - 1)P_0 + 1] \quad (4.16)$$

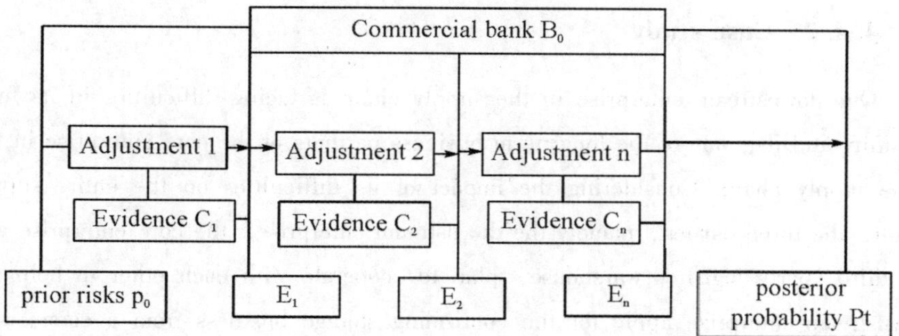

Fig. 4-3 Subjective Bayesian Relationship Figure of Confirming Storage Social Network in SME Supply Chain Financing

When the natural person B_0 continues to ask B_2 for information based on evidence C_2, he will also adjust his prior probability P_0. Then the posterior default probability will be:

$$P_{t2} = P(B_0/C_2) = LS_2 \cdot P_{t1} / [(LS_2 - 1)P_{t1} + 1] \quad (4.17)$$

Similarly, when the B_0 continues to ask Bn for information based on evidence C_n, the posterior default probability will be:

$$P_{tn} = P\ (B_0/Cn)\ = LS_N \cdot P_{t(n-1)} /\ [\ (LS_2 - 1)\ P_{t(n-1)} + 1] \quad (4.18)$$

Also, it can be computed through the subjective Bayesian simulation system of SME social network which is based on Simulink system. See Fig. 4-4.

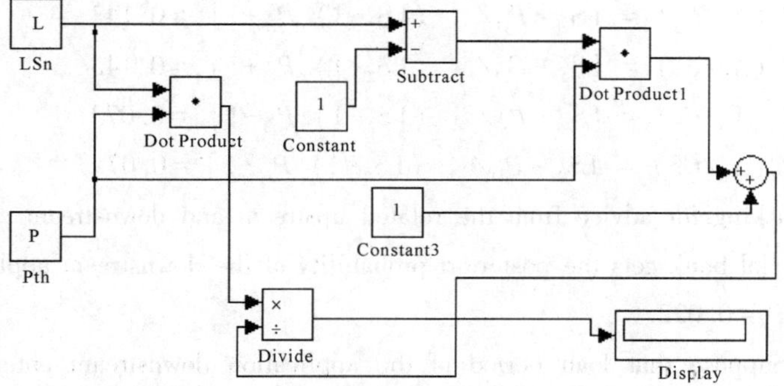

Fig. 4-4 Analysis of Social Network in Online Confirming Storage Business with Subjective Bayesian Simulation System

4.4.2 Case study

One downstream enterprise in the supply chain is facing difficulties in its fund liquidity and it is one of the long-term business partners of the core enterprise in the same supply chain. Considering the impact of its difficulties on the entire supply chain, the three parties, namely the downstream enterprise, the core enterprise and the third-party logistics warehouse, plan to cooperate with each other to help the downstream enterprise apply for the confirming storage business from a commercial bank. Assume that the loan amount is 1 million Yuan, the annual interest rate of the commercial bank is 10%, and the loan period is 6 months. Still suppose that the downstream enterprise has a good credit rating, with a priori probability (P_0) about 10%. After receiving the application for confirming storage business, the commercial bank carries out some investigations and some dynamic credit management of the downstream enterprise in the supply chain. It asks respectively the upstream businessman B_1, B_2, B_3, the core enterprise B_4 and the third-party logistics warehouse B_5 for some advice, and finally gets their default judgments of the downstream enterprise (LS_1, LN_1), (LS_2, LN_2) … (LS_5, LN_5) *as* (3, LN_1), (0.5, LN_2), (1, LN_3), (0.5, LN_4), (0.9, LN_5) respectively. Then, the following results can be attained through simulation and network analysis:

$$P_{t1}=P(X_0/C_1)=LS_1\cdot P_0/[(LS_1-1)P_0+1]=0.25 \quad (4.19)$$

$$P_{t2}=P(X_0/C_2)=LS_2\cdot P_{t1}/[(LS_2-1)P_{t1}+1]=0.143 \quad (4.20)$$

$$P_{t3}=P(X_0/C_3)=LS_2\cdot P_{t2}/[(LS_2-1)P_{t2}+1]=0.143 \quad (4.21)$$

$$P_{t4}=P(X_0/C_4)=LS_2\cdot P_{t3}/[(LS_2-1)P_{t3}+1]=0.073 \quad (4.22)$$

$$P_{t5}=P(X_0/C5)=LS_2\cdot P_{t4}/[(LS_2-1)P_{t4}+1]=0.07. \quad (4.23)$$

After asking for advice from the related upstream and downstream enterprises, the commercial bank gets the posteriori probability of the downstream application enterprise as $P_t=0.022$.

(1) Suppose that loan period of the application downstream enterprise is 6 months, then with an annual interest of 10%, the commercial bank's expected payoff will be: 1 (million) ×10%×6/12= 0.05 (million).

Considering the mortgage liquidity of the stock in the non-confirming storage business, the expected risk loss of the commercial bank will be: 1 (million) $X_{0.07}$ = 0.07 (million). Then it will turn out for the commercial bank that: the expected payoff<the expected loss. As a result the commercial bank will refuse the loan application of the downstream enterprise.

If considering that the confirming inventory can be liquidated in the warehouse business, and assuming a stock realizable discount rate of 0.7, the expected loss of commercial banks is: 1 (million) × (1−0.7) ×0.07= 0.021 (million). Then for the commercial bank, it will become the case that: the expected payoff > the expected loss. Thus, the commercial bank will accept the loan application of the downstream enterprise.

(2) From above we can see that if the loan amount of the commercial bank is M, the interest rate is r_0 and the discount rate is R_1, then:

The expected payoff for the commercial bank will be: $M \cdot r_0$

The expected loss for the commercial bank will be: $M \cdot P_{tn} \cdot (1-R_1)$

When $M \cdot r_0 > M \cdot P_{tn} \cdot (1-R_1)$ or $P_{tn} < r_0/(1-R_1)$, the commercial bank will accept the loan application of the confirmed SME in the supply chain.

When $M \cdot r_0 < M \cdot P_{tn} \cdot (1-R_1)$ or $P_{tn} > r_0/(1-R_1)$, the commercial bank will refuse the loan application of the confirmed SME in the supply chain.

Because R_1 is constantly changing along with the market ups and downs, the value of P_{tn} is also fluctuating. From the following figure one can see the commercial bank's strategies towards the SME applying for the confirming storage business.

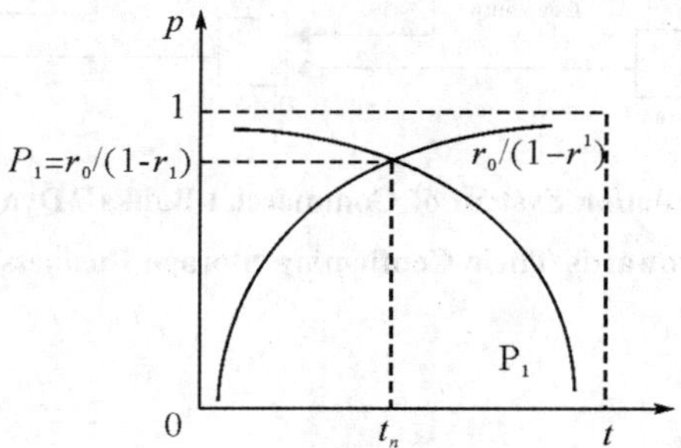

Fig. 4−5 **Dynamic Decisions of the Commercial Bank**

On the point of t_n, $P_{tn}=r_0/(1-R_1)$. This is the equilibrium point for the commercial bank's dynamic decisions. If P_{tn} continues to deviate down from the equilibrium point, and $r_0/(1-R_1)$ up, then the commercial bank will accept the loan application of the confirmed SME in the supply chain (as shown in Fig. 4−5). On the contrary, the commercial bank will refuse the corresponding loan application .

At the same time, we can also carry out a numeric simulation of the system with the software Simulink. Suppose that $LS=3$, $P=0.1$ and $r_0=0.1$. According to their different characteristics, the collateras fall into two kinds: the collaterals whose values fluctuate randomly with the changes of the market demand (for example: ships, vehicles, real-estate and so on) and the collaterals whose values decrease as time elapeses (for example : vegetable, fruit, fashionable clothes and so on). For the former, the input function of R_1 will be a random function with the fluctuation range of the pledged values being (0.2~0.65) (see Fig. 4-7); for the latter, the input function of R_1 will be a slope function with the slope being 0.09 (see Fig. 4-8). After simulation, we can see what is shown in Fig. 4-6~Fig. 4-8。

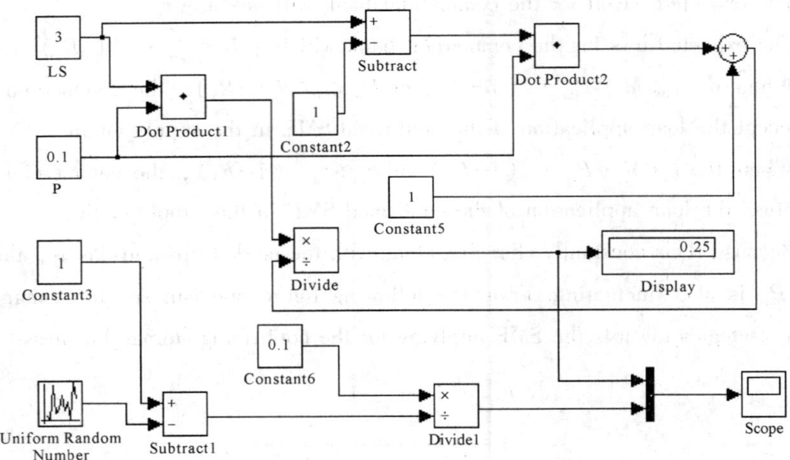

Fig. 4-6 Simulation System of Commercial Banks' Dynamic Decisions towards Their Confirming Storage Business

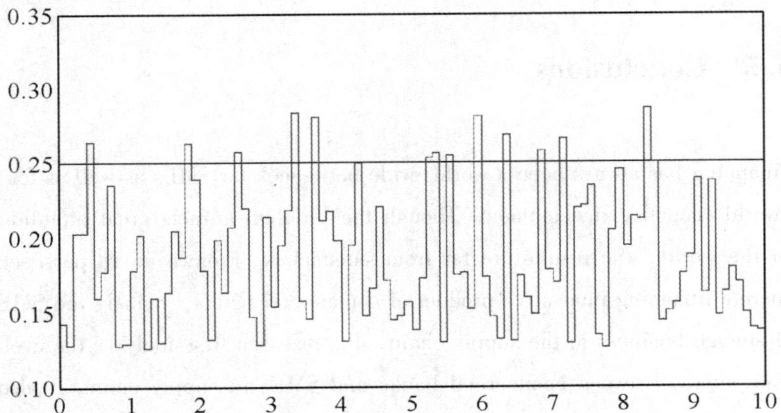

Fig. 4-7 Simulation of Dynamic Decisions When Inputting the Random Function

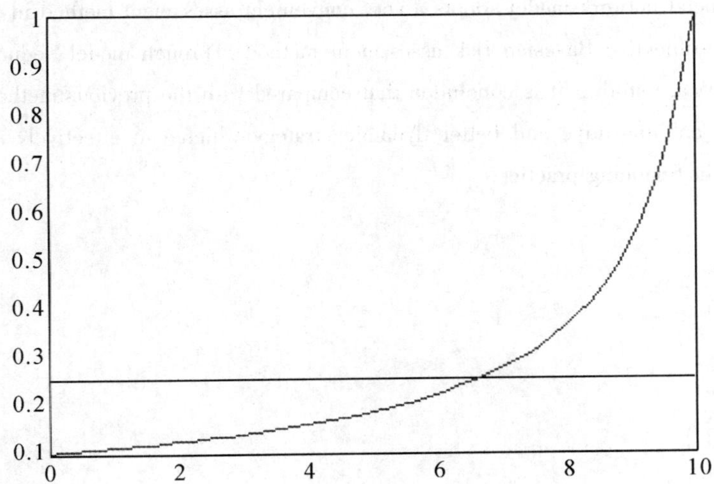

Fig. 4-8 Simulation of Dynamic Decisions When Inputting the Slope Function

As shown in Figs. 4-7 ~ Figs. 4-8, when the time series fluctuation curve is below the straight line, it is safe for the commercial banks to provide the online supply chain financing service to the SMEs. On the contrary, once the time series fluctuation curve is above the straight line, which means that there is a higher credit risk, the commercial banks should tighten or even cancel the confirming storage business to the SMEs so as to effectively control and prevent their credit risks.

4.5 Conclusions

Financing has always been a world-wide bottleneck for SMEs as well as for the overall world economic development. Though the problem attracts great attention from all over the world, the results are far from satisfactory. From a micro perspective of the concrete financing innovative product of commercial banks, namely the SME confirming storage business in the supply chain, the research first analyzes the evolutionary game process between commercial banks and SMEs in supply chain. It also tries hard to find out the game equilibrium and make judgment on whether they are the ESS point for the evolutionary game. Due to the fact that when the system is unstable, financing risk must be assessed for the confirming storage system, the resarch on the basis of social network model adopts a very convenient assessment method in the practice, the subjective Bayesian risk assessment method. Through model deduction and simulation case study, it is concluded that compared with the previous methods, this method is an innovative and better dynamic strategy which can effectively solve the problems in financing practice.

5 模式创新与风险控制论（三）：基于因子分析和系统动力学仿真对信用证结算风险的研究

5.1 文献综述

随着世界经济的全球化，各国之间的贸易往来日益频繁，贸易结算的使用工具也在不断深化。众所周知，信用证（L/C）是目前国际贸易活动中三大传统结算工具之一。特别是在初次贸易活动中，进出口双方一般不会采用T/T（电汇）、托收（D/P）结算工具，而信用证就往往承担了行使贸易结算工具的重要职责。但是这一活动具有复杂性、专业性、技术性等特点，特别是评估和计量不同国家、不同条款、不同人员、不同金融机构等的信用证结算风险，企业和个人往往很难对其进行系统性、动态性的把握。

前人对于信用证结算风险进行了有益的探索，国内外学者对于信用证的研究主要集中在以下几个视角：

（1）从商业银行面临的风险与收益的视角研究。

王玉珏（2012）研究了对于信用证打包放款产品商业银行可能面临的欺诈风险以及法律责任。杜庆霞（2014）认为信用证业务是商业银行低成本、高收益的业务。但是由于审单独立性原则，商业银行需要控制信息不对称所带来的风险。陈寰、林晓慧（2017）从开证行和融资行的角度，分析了如何管理大宗商品交易的信用证开证融资风险。南舒（2017）研究了结算行如何利用BP神经网络模型来防范信用证结算的风险。Rosmawani，CheHashim，Nurul Shahnaz Mahdzan（2014）研究了马来西亚商业银行的信用证结算业务。结果表明：商业银行一般会依照国际惯例UCP的相关规定，积极处理结算过程中参与人遇到的问题与风险事件。Friederike Niepmann，Tim Schmidt-Eisenlohr（2017）认为信用证结算可以减少商业银行贸易融资产品的风险。

（2）从国际贸易中进出口方企业风险的视角研究。

封文丽（2012）研究了出口信用证软条款风险的识别方法。王楚楚、周戈、王皓田（2013）通过举例说明了如何在国际贸易活动中防范信用证结算等风险。周凌轲、黄颖、王普玉（2018）从出口企业的角度研究了软条款风险的简便的识别方法。林璇华（2013）、李晓蕾（2018）等从我国进出口商的角度分析了信用证结算的各类风险，并提出了一些解决办法和措施。Hamed Alavi（2016）认为存在多个因素影响信用证结算风险，从企业角度研究了防范信用证欺诈的方法。Friederike Niepmann，Tim Schmidt-Eisenlohr（2018）用事实证明了信用证结算方式会正面影响美国企业的出口量。

（3）从国际惯例与法律风险防范的视角研究。

姜爱丽、王靖靖（2012）认为国内立法机关应该根据《跟单信用证统一惯例（UCP600）》制定相关的国内法律，来解决信用证欺诈问题。代兴军（2012）根据信用证独立性原则，研究了信用证欺诈的例外情况。张杨（2013）研究了国际惯例 UCP600 和 ISBP681 条文中的 18 项不足之处，并提出了一些建议。张晓微、姚新超（2016）根据国际商会有关的咨询回复文件，厘清了 UCP600 第 31 条和第 32 条的中英语言版本的理解差异。沈四宝、蒋琪（2018）针对信用证押汇业务，从司法角度解释和区分了押汇和议付的法律性质。Hamed Alavi（2016）从英国法律体系的角度阐释了跟单信用证各参与主体（进出口方、商业银行、法院等）的有限自主权力与责任界定。

（4）从新方法、新技术的视角：电子化、BPO、区块链技术的视角研究。

廖起平（2014）说明了国内商业银行在信用证结算方面已实现部分电子化操作，并进一步分析了未来采用全部电子化平台的原因、方向、可行性、流程等方面的问题。Turker Susmus，S. Ozgur Baslangic（2015）对比了传统结算方式并指出了它们的不足，指出了新方法 BPO（Bank Payment Obligation）在国际结算中的优势。王永梅（2017）研究了银行电子交单的特点、流程以及新问题等，并说明中信银行基于区块链的国内信用证信息传输系统（Block Chain based Letter of Credit System，BCLC）在 2017 年启动使用，改变了传统信用证的开立、传输、议付的方式。张鹏（2017）研究了区块链技术对信用证等传统结算业务的积极和负面影响。李丽琼（2017）展望了未来信用证在区块链技术的推动下的演化路径。

国内外学者对于信用证结算的研究较多，但大多数是基于定性的研究，定量的研究成果较少。本书采取定量的方法，基于探索性因子分析法挖掘影响信用证结算的主要风险因素，在此基础上，构建系统动力学因果图，描述风险因素之间的传递函数，撰写 Dynamo 方程，并通过系统动力学仿真来评估和控制信用证结算的动态风险。

5.2 基于探索性因子分析对信用证结算风险因素的研究

5.2.1 研究原理、方法及模型

信用证结算的影响因素是复杂的，观测变量之间往往存在着相关关系，关系紧密的变量可组成共同的公因子。利用探索性因子分析的方法可以挖掘出共同的公因子。

其分析模型如下：

（1）假设条件：

①公因子个数小于或者等于观测变量的个数。

②公因子与误差项不存在相关关系，特殊项的方差可以不同。

③公因子之间不存在相关关系，公因子的方差为 1。

（2）数学原理模型：

①$X=AF+\varepsilon$，即：

$X_1=a_{11}F_1+a_{12}F_1+\cdots\cdots+a_{1n}F_n+\varepsilon_1$

$X_2=a_{21}F_1+a_{22}F_1+\cdots\cdots+a_{2n}F_n+\varepsilon_2$

$X_3=a_{31}F_1+a_{32}F_1+\cdots\cdots+a_{3n}F_n+\varepsilon_3$

………

$X_n=a_{n1}F_1+a_{n2}F_1+\cdots\cdots+a_{nn}F_n+\varepsilon_n$

②观测变量为 $X=(X_1, X_2, X_3 \ldots\ldots X_i)$，公因子为 $F=(F_1, F_2, F_3, \ldots\ldots F_n)$，特殊项为 $\varepsilon=(\varepsilon_1, \varepsilon_2, \varepsilon_3 \ldots\ldots \varepsilon_n)$。

（3）公因子的提取：

利用 SPSS 软件计算公因子贡献率，根据特征值大小提取公因子。

5.2.2 信用证风险影响因素分析

闵感（2007）将信用证风险归纳为合同风险、软条款风险、伪造信用证风险、银行信用风险、单证风险。张守红（2008）将信用证风险分为信用风险、单证风险、市场风险、法律风险、欺诈风险。凌智（2008）将信用证风险分为单证

风险、价格风险、软条款风险、法律风险、操作流程风险。李蕴萍（2009）把信用证风险分为软条款风险、操作风险、价格风险、市场风险、资金风险、汇率风险、政治风险、虚假单证风险。李楠（2010）把信用证涉及的风险分为外部宏观环境风险（汇率、贸易摩擦、国际惯例、国家政策）和微观环境影响风险（当事人的信用状况、合同条款风险、单据风险、操作流程风险）。

根据对以上研究以及其他资料的归纳总结，并征求相关业务操作人员的意见，制作出表5-1，通过问卷调查，提交外贸业务经理和理论研究者对量表的内容效度进行评价。

表 5-1　信用证风险指标选取

风险一级指标	风险二级指标	指标描述与解释
信用证	合同条款风险 X1	涉及公司名称、交易价格、地点、包装等。
	提单条款风险 X2	单份或多份正本提单径（直）寄开证申请人，买方可能持此单先行将货提走。 记名提单：承运人可能会仅凭收货人的合法身份证明交货，而不要求提交提单。
软条款	签字印章条款风险 X3	信用证中出现与“兑付时须由开证申请人签字，且签字盖章须与银行留底相符”类似的条款而造成的风险。
	检验条款风险 X4	信用证规定“只有由申请人或其指定的签字人验货并签署质量检验合格证书，才能付款或生效”。
	装运条款风险 X5	由类似“有关运输事项如船名、装船日期、装卸港等以申请人修改后的通知为准”的条款引起的风险；由信用证中限制运输船只、船龄或航线等条款引起的风险。
	生效条款风险 X6	因条款规定“信用证暂时不生效，何时生效由银行另行通知；进口方收到他人货款后生效；货款须于货物运抵目的地经外汇管理局核准后付款”等造成的风险。
	矛盾条款风险 X7	前后条款互相矛盾，受益人无论如何也达不到单单一致；如一方面规定允许提交联运提单，另一方面又规定禁止转船。
	操作人员风险 X8	由经理、业务员、制单员、银行人员、单证审查员（虚假信用证）带来的风险。

表5-1(续)

风险一级指标	风险二级指标	指标描述与解释
操作	操作系统风险 X9	由谈判系统、IT 软件系统、银行电子系统问题引起的风险。
	外部事件影响 X13	信用证结算的外部环境如政治、经济、社会环境的变化引起了结算风险的产生。
	客户信用变动风险 X10	客户交易历史记录、资产负债状况等发生变化造成的风险
	法律环境变动风险 X11	信用证 UPC、配额限制、WTO 政策法规变化导致的风险。
	经济环境变动风险 X12	金融危机、汇率、税收、经济共同体的形成与发展带来的风险。
微、宏观环境	政治环境变动影响 X14	总统、首相等领导人的更替、地区局势的变动引发的风险。
	文化环境变动影响 X15	英美文化、亚洲儒家文化、伊斯兰文化等交替带来的风险。

许多研究者认为外部事件影响指标 X13 与经济环境变化 X12、法律环境变化 X11 之间相关程度高、重合度大；政治环境变动影响 X14、文化环境变动影响 X15 都是通过影响法律环境变动风险 X11、经济环境变化 X12 来对信用证结算产生影响。通过无记名投票，采用德尔菲实验方法经过几次反复测验，最终建议取消外部事件影响 X13 和政治环境变动影响 X14、文化环境变动影响 X15 三项变量指标。

5.2.3 信用证风险探索性因子分析

问卷调查：共发放问卷 300 份，通过电子邮件和实地发放问卷的方法，共回收问卷 220 份，回收率为 73%，大于 30%的回收率要求，说明该问卷调查的回收率在有效值范围内。

（1）KMO 和 Bartlett's 球形检验：KMO 测试简单相关系数和偏相关系数，Bartlett's 球形检验测试样本数据的分布特征和独立情况。运用 SPSS 统计软件对数据进行分析，测得结果为 KMO 等于 0.781，该值大于 Kaiser 所规定的 0.5，因此可以进行因子分析；卡方值为 1 737.927；自由度为 66；相伴概率为 0，小于 0.000 1，拒绝变量为单位阵的假设。说明该数据适合因子分析。

表 5-2 KMO 和 Bartlett's 球形检验结果

KMO 和 Bartlett's 检验		
KMO 抽样充分性		0.781
Bartlett's 球形检验	Approx. Chi-Square	1 737.927
	df	66
	Sig.	0.000

（2）公因子提取效果：通过 SPSS 软件分析变量与各个因子间的相互关系，可以得到各个变量在各个因子上的载荷量，载荷量的大小表示两者之间的关联程度。如果 Factor loading 越大，则相关程度越高，一般小于 0.5 的载荷量表示相关程度不明显，可以删除。本书的实证分析采用关联矩阵（correlation matrix）并进行特征值提取（based on Eigen value extract），然后采用最大方差法旋转，得到表 5-3 的因子负荷矩阵。从表中可以看出，*X*1、*X*2、*X*3、*X*4、*X*5、*X*6、*X*7 七个变量在因子 *F*1 上的载荷量均大于 0.7，*X*10、*X*11、*X*12 三个变量在因子 *F*2 上的载荷量均大于 0.6，*X*8、*X*9 两个变量在因子 *F*3 上的载荷量均大于 0.7。

表 5-3 因子方差负荷矩阵

风险指标	*F*1	*F*2	*F*3
提单条款风险 *X*1	0.894	0.185	-0.121
合同条款风险 *X*2	0.868	0.293	0.047
签字印章条款风险 *X*3	0.932	0.101	0.130
检验条款风险 *X*4	0.809	0.210	0.286
装运条款风险 *X*5	0.910	0.124	0.133
生效条款风险 *X*6	0.815	0.346	0.234
矛盾条款风险 *X*7	0.736	0.427	0.326
操作人员风险 *X*8	0.139	0.167	0.791
操作系统风险 *X*9	0.118	-0.083	0.914
客户信用变动风险 *X*10	0.210	0.900	0.200
法律环境变动风险 *X*11	0.183	0.819	-0.264
经济环境变动风险 *X*12	0.410	0.649	0.298

（3）公因子提取和命名：

表 5-4　　因子特征值与方差贡献率

Total Variance Explained									
N	Initial Eigenvalues			Extraction Sums of Squared Loadings			Rotation Sums of Squared Loadings		
	Total	% of Variance	Cumulative %	Total	% of Variance	Cumulative %	Total	% of Variance	Cumulative %
1	6. 756	56. 296	56. 296	6. 756	56. 296	56. 296	5. 434	45. 286	45. 286
2	1. 667	13. 893	70. 189	1. 667	13. 893	70. 189	2. 406	20. 054	65. 340
3	1. 397	11. 639	81. 828	1. 397	11. 639	81. 828	1. 979	16. 488	81. 828
4	0. 602	5. 018	86. 846						
5	0. 416	3. 464	90. 310						
6	0. 286	2. 387	92. 697						
7	0. 281	2. 345	95. 041						
8	0. 196	1. 630	96. 671						
9	0. 174	1. 452	98. 123						
10	0. 116	0. 970	99. 093						
11	0. 069	0. 577	99. 671						
12	0. 040	0. 329	100. 00						

Extraction Method：Principal Component Analysis.

表 5-4 为因子特征值与方差贡献率。由此可见，第一个公因子的特征值为 6. 756，旋转后为 5. 434；方差贡献率旋转前为 56. 296%，旋转后为 45. 286%，包含的变量为：提单条款风险、签字印章条款风险、保险条款风险、检验条款风险、装运条款风险、生效条款风险、矛盾条款风险，它们都是反映信用证自身条款的风险。第二个公因子的特征值为 1. 667，旋转后为 2. 406；方差贡献率旋转前为 13. 893%，旋转后为 20. 054%，包含操作人员风险、操作系统风险，反映的是信用证操作过程中银行、进出口企业人员的操作风险。第三个公因子的特征值为 1. 397，旋转后为 1. 979；方差贡献率旋转前为 11. 639%，旋转后为 16. 488%，包含客户信用变动风险、经济环境变动风险、法律环境变动风险，它们说明的是信用证结算中微观、宏观环境风险因素。三个公因子的特征值都大于 1，累积贡献率为 81. 828%，可以看出 *F*1、*F*2、*F*3 三个因子基本上反映了全部指标的信息，结果符合预先拟定的因子分析模型。

因子命名：根据公因子 *F*1 包含的变量，可以将 *F*1 命名为条款风险；同理，*F*2 命名为操作风险，*F*3 命名为环境风险（企业信用风险、国家风险）。

5.3 信用证风险系统动力学仿真分析

在对信用证风险因素的探索性因子研究的基础上，我们可以构建系统动力学因果图，并通过动力学仿真来评估和控制风险。

传统的对信用证系统风险的研究主要是从单个系统去评价信用证的风险，比如通过单证系统、进出口商业银行系统、环境系统等其中一个或者几个系统，很少有人把几者整合起来形成复杂的系统进行研究。系统动力学研究能够在一些方面克服这些研究的不足。

图 5-1 是系统动力学仿真的一般流程，它把系统看成是多重信息反馈系统。研究人员对系统进行深入的分析，把系统分解成不同的因素集合，然后将不同的因素集合联系起来建立起因果关系反馈图，并通过 Vensim 软件建立系统流程图（包括 Dynamo 方程的建立与输入），最后对现实的系统结构进行仿真实验，以找出较优的系统结构。

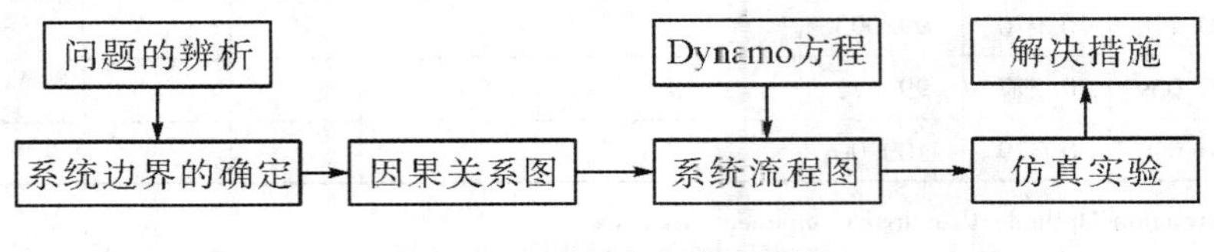

图 5-1 系统动力学流程图

5.3.1 模型设计与参数设置

5.3.1.1 国际贸易中信用证结算风险系统的因果关系图设计

（1）首先，对问题进行辨析：

信用证结算风险评价系统是一个复杂的系统。根据探索性因子分析的结果，我们可以把它分为四类风险因素子系统：国家风险子系统、企业信用风险子系统、操作风险子系统、条款风险子系统。各个子系统也可分为若干个子子系统，主要包括国家概况风险系统、政治风险系统，经济风险系统、投资风险系统、双边关系风险系统、操作流程风险系统、操作人员风险系统、操作系统风险系统、外部事件风险系统、道德风险系统、负债风险系统、资产风险系统、有效期风险系统、交单期风险系统、装船期风险系统、商检风险系统、提单风险系统、生效条件风险系统、付款条件风险系统等。

我们可以通过以下示意图来认识各因素之间的关系：

从图 5-2 中可以清楚地看出 A 到 C 层上信用证风险之间的逻辑关系，不同层次上的因素可以通过函数联系起来。

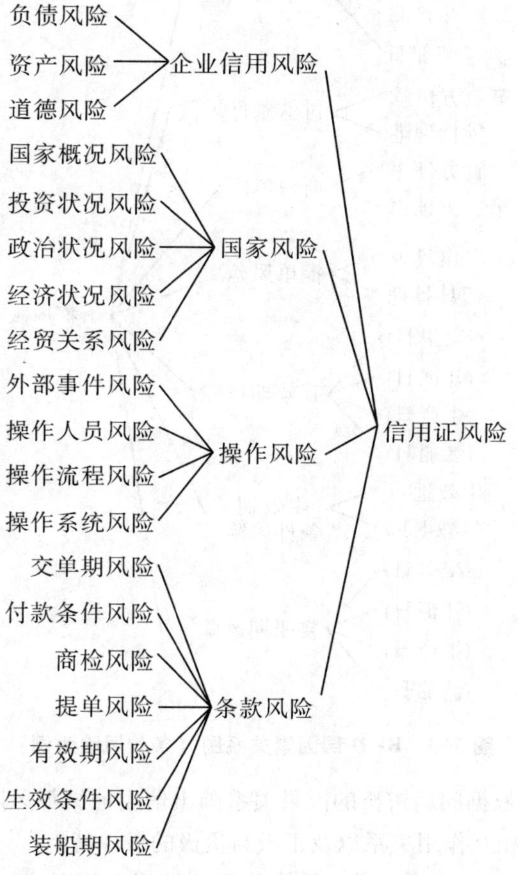

图 5-2 **A～C 层因素关系图**

同理，从图 5-3 中可以清楚地看出 B 层条款风险到 D 层因素之间的逻辑关系，因素与层次之间可以通过各种函数关系进行传递。

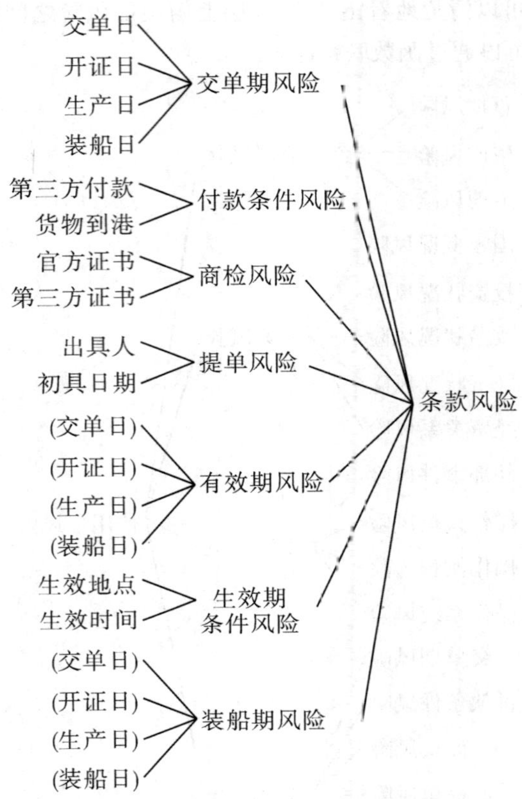

图 5-3　**B~D 层因素关系图（条款风险为例）**

（2）其次，根据问题辨析的因果关系画出信用证结算风险的因果关系图，注意因素之间的相互作用关系以及正极与负极的极性特点。

从图 5-4 中可以清楚地看出整个信用证结算风险影响因素系统的构造特点，同时也可以看出因素之间的作用原理以及因素之间的极性关系。

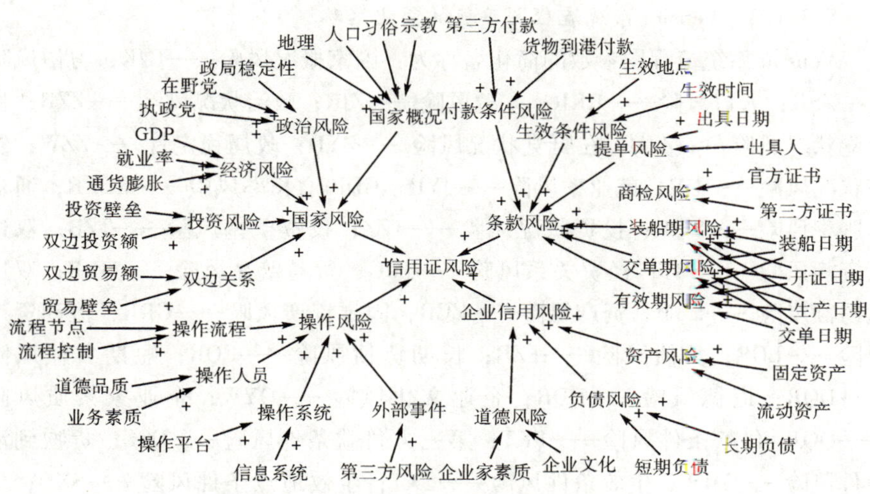

图 5-4 信用证风险系统因果关系图

5.3.1.2 在信用证结算风险的因果关系图的基础上利用 Vensim 画出系统流程图

通过因果关系图厘清变量之间的关系，通过洞、流量、变量、辅助变量等把各个风险因素有机地联系起来。

从图 5-5 中可以清楚地看出信用证风险系统流程图的洞、流量、变量、辅助变量等之间的关系，为下一步写 Dynamo 方程和系统仿真打下了基础。

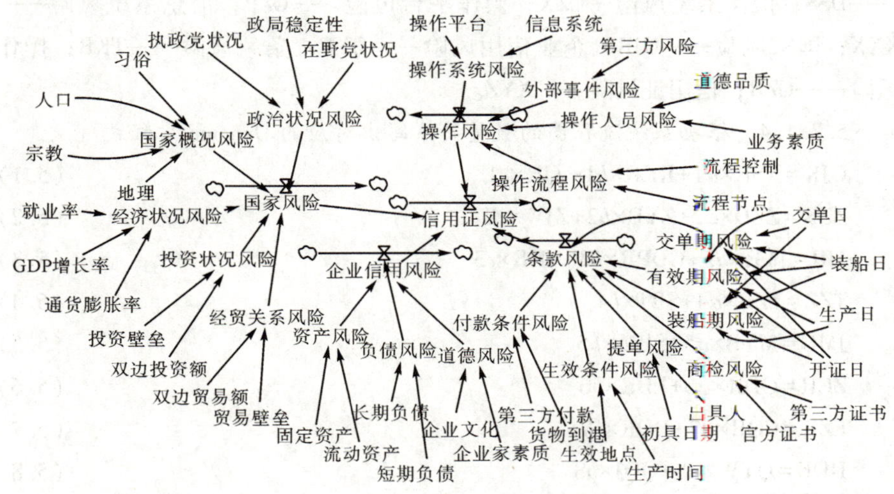

图 5-5 信用证风险系统流程图

5.3.1.3 Vensim 系统流程图参数的简化名称

Vensim 系统流程图参数的简化名称为：国家概况风险——GJK；习俗风险——XSR；人口风险——RKR；宗教风险——ZJR；政治状况风险——ZZR；执政党状况风险——ZZD；在野党状况风险——ZYD；政局稳定性——ZZW；经济状况风险——JJR；就业率风险——JYR；GDP 增长率风险——GDPR；通货膨胀率风险——THR；投资状况风险——TZZ；投资壁垒风险——TZB；双边投资额风险——SBT；经贸关系风险——JMG；贸易壁垒风险——MYB；双边贸易额风险——SBM；资产风险——ZCR；固定资产风险——GDR；流动资产风险——LDR；负债风险——FZR；长期负债风险——CQR；短期负债风险——DQR；道德风险——DDR；企业文化风险——QYW；企业家素质风险——QQJ；付款条件风险——FKT；第三方付款条件风险——DSF；货物到港条件风险——HDF；生效条件风险——SXT；生效地点条件风险——SXD；生效时间条件风险——SXS；提单风险——TDF；提单出具日期风险——TDR；提单出具人风险——TDC；商检风险——SJF；官方商检证书风险——GFS；第三方商检证书风险——DSF；装船期风险——ZCQ；有效期风险——YXQ；交单期风险——JDQ；生产日期风险——SCR；开证日期风险—KZR；装船日期风险——ZCR；交单日期风险——JDR；操作流程风险——CZL；流程控制风险——LCK；流程节点风险——LCJ；操作人员风险——CZR；道德品质风险——DDP；业务素质风险——YWS；外部事件风险——WBS；第三方事件风险——DSS；操作系统风险—CZX；操作平台风险——CZP；信息系统风险——XXX；国家风险——GJR；企业信用风险——QYC；条款风险——TKR；操作风险——CZR；信用证风险——XYZ。

5.3.1.4 根据系统流程图的数量关系写出对应的 Dynamo 方程式

$$GJK=XSR\times a1+RKR\times b1+ZJR\times c1 \tag{5.1}$$

$$ZZR=ZZD\times a2+ZYD\times b2+ZJW\times c2 \tag{5.2}$$

$$JJR=JYR\times a3+GDPR\times b3+THR\times c3 \tag{5.3}$$

$$TZZ=TZB\times a4+SBT\times b4 \tag{5.4}$$

$$JMG=MYB\times a5+SBM\times b5 \tag{5.5}$$

$$ZCR=GDR\times a6+LDR\times b6 \tag{5.6}$$

$$FZR=CQR\times a7+DQR\times b7 \tag{5.7}$$

$$DDR=QYW\times a8+QQJ\times b8 \tag{5.8}$$

$$FKT=DSF\times a9+HDF\times b9 \tag{5.9}$$

$$SXT=SXD\times a10+SXS\times b10 \tag{5.10}$$

$$TDF = TDR \times a11 + TDC \times b11 \tag{5.11}$$

$$SJF = GFS \times a12 + DSF \times b12 \tag{5.12}$$

$$ZCQ = SCR \times a13 + KZR \times b13 + ZCR \times c13 + JDR \times d13 \tag{5.13}$$

$$YXQ = SCR \times a14 + KZR \times b14 + ZCR \times c14 + JDR \times d14 \tag{5.14}$$

$$JDQ = SCR \times a15 + KZR \times b15 + ZCR \times c15 + JDR \times d15 \tag{5.15}$$

$$CZL = LCK \times a16 + LCJ \times b16 \tag{5.16}$$

$$CZR = DDP \times a17 + YWS \times b17 \tag{5.17}$$

$$WBS = DSS \times a18 \tag{5.18}$$

$$CZX = CZP \times a19 + XXX \times b19 \tag{5.19}$$

$$GJR = GJK \times e1 + ZZR \times f1 + JJR \times g1 + TZZ \times h1 + JMG \times i1 \tag{5.20}$$

$$QYC = ZCR \times e2 + FZR \times f2 + DDR \times g2 \tag{5.21}$$

$$TKR = FKT \times e3 + SXT \times f3 + TDF \times g3 + SJF \times h3 + ZCQ \times i3 + YXQ \times j3 + JDQ \times k3 \tag{5.22}$$

$$CZR = CZL \times e4 + CZR \times f4 + WBS \times g4 + CZX \times h4 \tag{5.23}$$

$$XYZ = GJR \times L + QYC \times M + TKR \times N + CZR \times O \tag{5.24}$$

（$e1$，$e2$，$e3$……；$f1$，$f2$，$f3$……；$g1$，$g2$，$g3$……；$h1$，$h2$，$h3$……；$i1$，$i2$，$i3$……；$j1$，$j2$，$j3$……；$k1$，$k2$，$k3$……；L，M，N 分别代表相应各指标的权重大小）

5.3.2 对系统模型进行仿真分析

5.3.2.1 系统模型假设

为了便于对信用证结算系统风险的波动有一个直观的认识，我们对系统进行简化处理，提出一些假设条件。

（1）假设信用证结算系统中各参与主体都是理性经济人，他们的目标都是追求同等风险条件下的利润最大化。

（2）除了执政党状况风险、政局稳定性风险、短期负债风险三个参数波动服从不同的分布外，将信用证结算的各个子系统、子子系统的各参数的起初目标值设定为 0。

5.3.2.2 信用证结算风险系统的仿真实验分析

利用计算机进行仿真实验：设置 initial time 为 0，final time 为 100 months，步长为 1 个月。

初始设置：

FINAL TIME = 100

Units：Month

The final time for the simulation

INITIAL TIME = 0

Units：Month

The final time for the simulation

SAVEPER = TIME STEP

Units：Month ［0，100］

The frequency with which output is stored

Time STEP = 1

Units：Month ［0，100］

The time step for simulation

从图 5-6 至图 5-9 中可以看出：D 层风险因素——执政党状况风险、政局稳定性风险服从不同数值分布，而二者波动之间相互影响会形成 C 层风险因素——政治状况风险的波动。B 层风险因素——国家风险波动、C 层风险因素——政治状况风险的波动与 D 层风险因素——执政党状况风险波动以及 D 层——政局稳定性风险的波动形态具有部分相似性：它们具有一定的内在联系。但是风险波动的幅度与峰值有所不同，这说明系统风险同时受集聚效应和分散效应的影响。

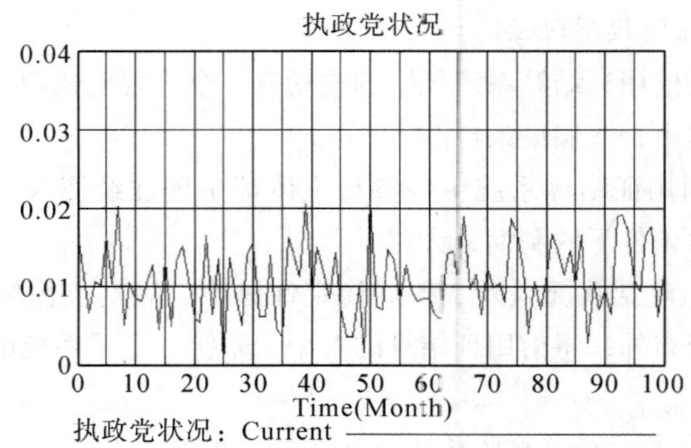

图 5-6 执政党状况风险波动

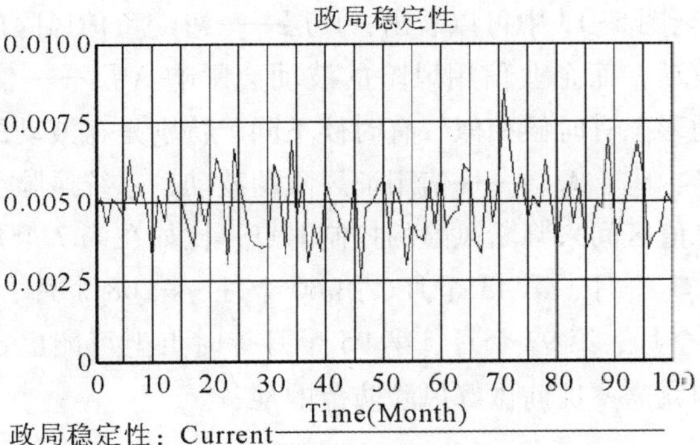

图 5-7　政局稳定性风险波动

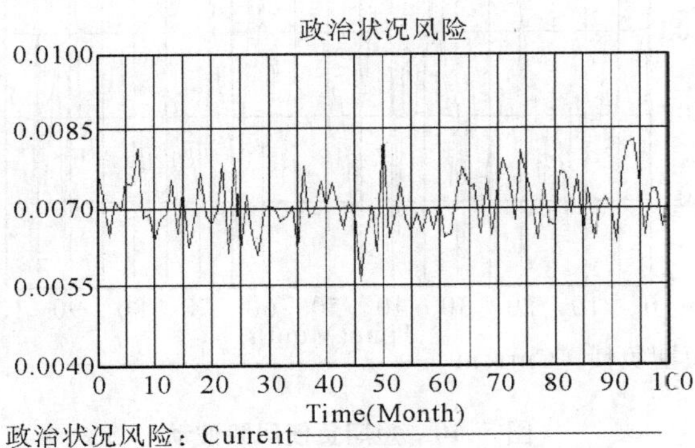

图 5-8　政治状况风险波动

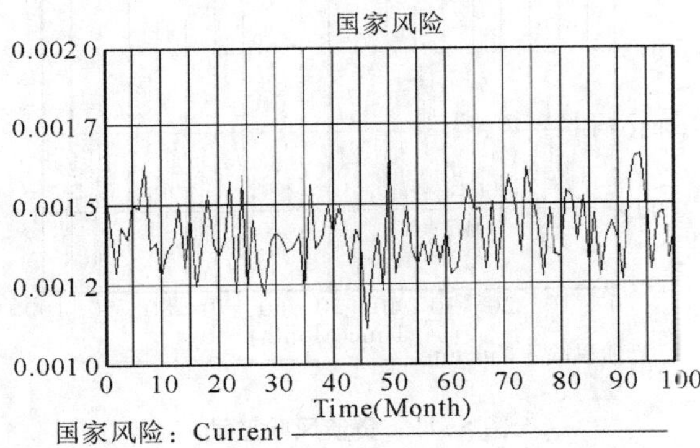

图 5-9　国家风险波动

从图 5-10 至图 5-13 中可以看出：D 层——短期负债风险的波动会影响企业信用风险的波动，而企业信用风险的波动会影响 A 层——信用证风险的波动。它们的波动形态有时候相似、有时候不同，特别是在波动的振幅和峰值上存在明显的差异。基于 A 层——信用证风险的波动，系统风险分析人员可以通过观察系统的峰值区间来判断风险的控制时点，比如在第 7 个月、第 20 个月、第 27 个月、第 37 个月、第 43 个月、第 60 个月、第 68 个月、第 76 个月、第 82 个月、第 89 个月、第 92 个月、第 95 个月等时点上可能出现峰值，那么企业或者金融机构就需要提前做好风险防范的准备。

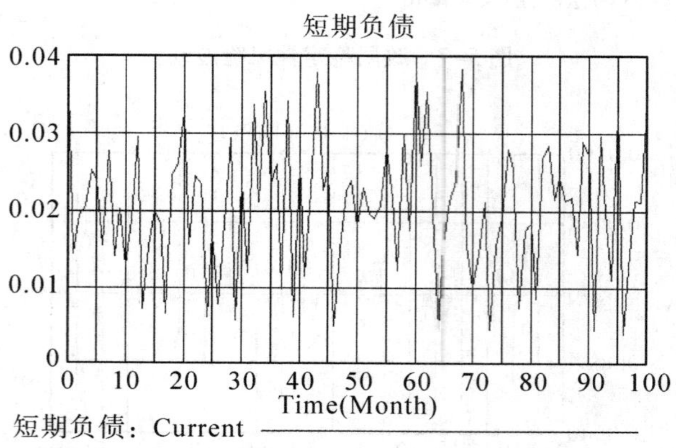

图 5-10　短期负债风险波动

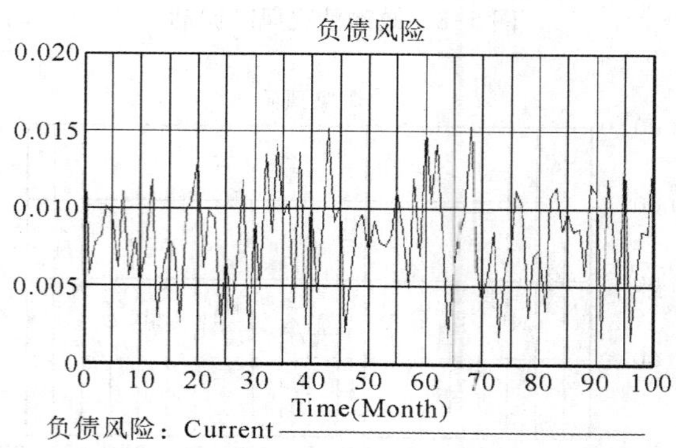

图 5-11　负债风险波动

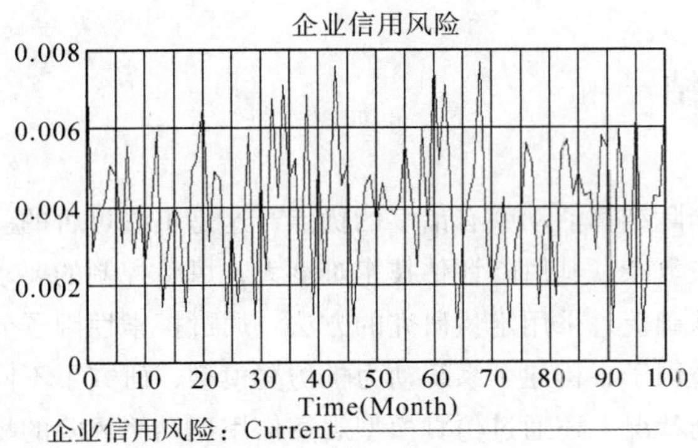

图 5-12　企业信用风险波动

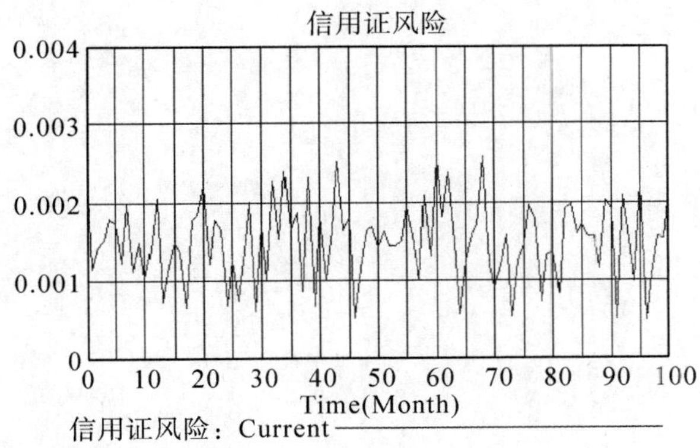

图 5-13　信用证风险波动

通过信用证结算系统的仿真结果可以看出，系统中的每一个层次的每一细小风险因素的变动都会引起信用证风险的波动，只是由于反应函数与传导机制的差别，最终风险波动的大小和方向就会存在差异。所以，在评估信用证结算风险系统的时候，既要关注每个层级中各个风险因素的变动情况，又要关注系统之间风险的大小。当在某一个时刻信用证风险的大小即将达到峰值的时候，我们就可以采取多种方法进行防控，比如采用一些基于出口信用保险的方法来防范信用证结算风险，确保系统性风险发生时能得到有效的控制。

5.4 总结

信用证在国际结算活动中有诸多的优点，这是不置可否的。但是信用证在使用上相对比较复杂，其风险评估技术难度大，风险控制的要求高。本书在前人定性研究的基础上，采用定量研究的方法。通过探索性因子分析提取了信用证结算风险的公因子，构建了系统动力学仿真模型，研究了不同参数条件下信用证风险的波动状况。还通过仿真模型观察信用证结算风险的峰值情况，并提出了及时有效地防控可能出现的信用证结算风险的方法。

5 Model Innovation and Theory of Risk Control (Ⅲ): Researchon Risks of Letter of Credit Settlement Based on Factor Analysis and System Dynamics Simulation

5.1 Literature Review

With globalization of the world economy and the frequent exchanges of trade among countries, the settlement tools become more and more advanced. As is known to all, letter of credit (L/C) is one of the three traditional settlement instruments in international trade currently. Especially in the first time of trade, as the import and export parties generally will not adopt some risky settlement tools such as T/T (telegraphic transfer) and D/P (document against payment), L/C will often assume the important responsibility of exercising the "the first night right". However, as L/C settlement is usually featured by complexity, professionality and technicality, companies and individuals often find it difficult to grasp the risks systematically and dynamically, especially when facing the assessment and measurement problems of the L/C settlement risks of different countries, different contract clauses, different people and different financial institutions.

Researchers have carried out some beneficial explorations to the L/C settlement risks. Studies of L/C in and out of China are mainly carried out from the following perspectives.

(1) the perspective of risks faced by and payoffs of the commercial banks.

Wang Yujue (2012) studies the possible fraud risks and legal liability faced by commercial banks when adopting the L/C packing loan product. Du Qingxia (2014) thinks that the L/C business is one of the low-cost and high-yield businesses of commercial banks. Nevertheless, due to the independence principle of documents examination, commercial banks need to control the risks caused by asymmetric information. Chen Huan, Lin Xiaohui (2017) analyzes how opening and financing banks manage the opening and financing risks of L/C in bulk commodity transactions. Nan Shu (2017) studies how the clearing banks use BP neural network model to prevent the L/C settlement risks. Rosmawani, CheHashim, Nurul Shahnaz Mahdzan (2014) studies the L/C settlement business of commercial banks in Malaysia. The results show that commercial banks generally follow the relevant provisions of the international practice UCP and they also actively deal with the problems and risk events encountered by participants in the settlement processes. Friederike Niepmann, Tim Schmidt - Eisenlohr (2017) thinks that L/C settlement can help reduce the risks brought by the commercial banks' trade financing products.

(2) the perspective of risks faced by the importers and exporters in international trade.

Feng Wenli (2012) tells about the identification methods of the soft clause risks in export L/Cs. Wang Chuchu, Zhou Ge, Wang Haotian (2013) illustrates with examples how to prevent L/C settlement risks in international trade. Zhou Lingke, Huang Ying; Wang Puyu (2018) provides the simple identification methods of soft clause risks from the viewpoint of export enterprise. Lin Xuanhua, Li Xiaolei (2018) analyzes the various risks in the L/C settlement from the viewpoint of China's importers and exporters and brings out some solutions. Hamed Alavi (2016) considers that there are lots of factors which can cause the L/C settlement risks. It also puts forward some methods for preventing L/C fraud risks from the enterprise angle. Friederike Niepmann, Tim Schmidt-Eisenlohr (2018) proves with facts that L/C settlement method has a positive effect on the export volume of U. S. enterprises.

(3) the perspective of international practice and legal risk prevention.

Jang Aili, Wang Jingjing (2012) thinks that the China's legislature should formulate relevant laws in accordance with the Uniform Practice of Documentary Credit (UCP600) to resolve the problem of L/C fraud. De Xingjun (2012) studies some uncommon L/C fraud cases based on the L/C independence principle. Zhang Yang

(2013) researches on 18 deficiencies of the provisions in the international practice UCP600 and ISBP681 and also puts forward some suggestions. Zhang Xiaowei, Yao Xinchao (2016) makes clear the understanding differences between the English and Chinese versions of the 31st and 32nd provisions of UCP600 based on the consultation reply documents of the International Chamber of Commerce. Targeting at the L/C bill purchase, Shen Sibao, Jiang Qi (2018) distinguishes between the legal natures of bill purchase and negotiation from the judicial angle. Hamed Alavi (2016) explains the limited autonomous power and responsibility boundary for the participants (importers, exporters, commercial banks, courts, etc.) of the documentary L/C from the angle of English legal system.

(4) the perspective of new methods and new technologies: electronization, BPO and block-chain technology.

Liao Qiping (2014) shows that commercial banks in China have already realized partial electronization in the operations of L/C settlement. It also goes on to analyze the reasons, direction, feasibility, process and so on of adopting the comprehensive electronic platform in the future. Turker Susmus, S. Ozgur Baslargic (2015) compares traditional settlement methods and points out their shortcomings, after which it also talks about the advantages of the new method BPO (Bank Payment Obligation) in international settlement. Wang Yongmei (2017) studies the characteristics, process, and new problems of banks' e-delivery. She also shows the readers that China's CITIC Bank has launched its Block Chain Based L/C System (BCLC) in 2017 which changes the opening, transmitting, negotiating ways of the traditional L/C. Zhang Peng (2017) studies the positive and negative effects exerted by block chain technology on traditional settlement services such as L/C. Li Liqiong (2017) forecasts the evolutionary path of future L/C under the impetus of block chain technology.

To sum up, scholars worldwide have done lots of researches on L/C settlement, but most of them are qualitative rather than quantitative. This research, based on the quantitative methods and exploratory factor analysis, finds out the main risk factors which affect the L/C settlement. What's more, it also constructs a system dynamics (SD) causes tree, which describes the transfer function between risk factors. Furthermore, it sets up dynamo equations as well as tries to assess and control the dynamic risks of L/C settlement through SD simulation.

5.2 Research on Risk Factors of L/C Settlement Based on Exploratory Factor Analysis

5.2.1 Research Principles, Methods and Models

Lots of factors can affect the L/C settlement and there is often a correlation between the observation variables. The closely related variables together can make up a common factor which can be mined by exploratory factor analysis.

The analytical model is as follows:

(1) Assumptions.

①The number of the common factors is less than or equal to the number of the observed variables.

②There is no correlation between the common factors and error terms, with variance of special terms being possibly different.

③There is no correlation among the common factors, and variance of the common factors is 1.

(2) Mathematical principle model.

①$X = AF+\varepsilon$.

i. e.: $X_1 = a_{11}F_1+a_{12}F_1+\ldots\ldots+a_{1n}F_n+\varepsilon_1$

$X_2 = a_{21}F_1+a_{22}F_1+\ldots\ldots+a_{2n}F_n+\varepsilon_2$

$X_3 = a_{31}F_1+a_{32}F_1+\ldots\ldots+a_{3n}F_n+\varepsilon$

………

$X_n = a_{n1}F_1+a_{n2}F_1+\ldots\ldots+a_{nn}F_n+\varepsilon_n$

②The observation variables: $X=(X_1, X_2, X_3\cdots\cdots X_i)$; the common variables: $F=(F_1, F_2, F_3, \ldots\ldots F_n)$; the special terms: $\varepsilon=(\varepsilon_1, \varepsilon_2, \varepsilon_3\cdots\cdots\varepsilon_n)$.

(3) Extraction of the common factors.

The contribution rates of the common factors are calculated with SPSS software, and the common factors are extracted according to the Eigen values.

5.2.2 Analysis of the Influencing Factors of L/C Risks

Min Gan (2007) divides the L/C risks into the contract risk, the soft clause risk, the forged L/C, the bank credit risk and the document risk. Zhang Shouhong

(2008) groups the L/C risks into the credit risk, the document risk, the market risk, the legal risk and the fraud risk. Within Ling Zhi (2008), L/C risks fall into the document risk, the price risk, the soft clause risk, the legal risk and the operation process risk. Li Yunping (2009) divides the L/C risks into the soft clause risk, the operation risk, the price risk, the market risk, the capital risk, the exchange rate risk, the political risk as well as the forged document risk. Li Nan (2010) groups the L/C risks into risks caused by external macro environment (exchange rate, trade friction, international practice, national policy) and risks caused by internal micro environment (participants' credit status, risks of contract terms, document risks, and operation process risks).

After summarizing the above researches and some other information as well as consulting the relevant business operators, the following table is made, after which it is also submitted to some foreign trade managers and theoretical researchers to have the validity of its content evaluated.

Table 5-1 Parameters of L/C Risks

1st level risk parameters	2nd level risk parameters	description and interpretation of the parameters
L/C	risks caused by the contract provisions: *X*1	risks that are related to the company name, transaction price, location, packing, and so on.
	risks caused by the B/L clauses: *X*2	(a) risks caused when one or more copies (there are three copies altogether) of the original B/L is/are directly sent to the applicant (the buyer), by which the buyer may take the goods away on ahead; (b) risks caused when it is a straight B/L: the carrier may deliver the goods on the basis of the legal identity of the consignee without asking for the original B/L.

Table5-1(续)

1st level risk parameters	2nd level risk parameters	description and interpretation of the parameters
soft clauses	risks caused by the signature and seal affixation clauses: $X3$	risks caused by soft clauses such as "signature should be made by the applicant"; or "the signature and seal must be in accordance with the copy in the bank".
	risk caused by inspection clauses: $X4$	risks caused by clauses such as "only when the applicant or his designated signatory has inspected the goods and signed the certificate of inspection will the L/C come into effect and the payment be paid".
	risks caused by shipment clauses: $X5$	(a) risks caused by clauses such as "matters of shipment such as the name of the ship, the date of shipment, the ports of loading and unloading should be subject to the modified notice of the applicant"; (b) in the L/C there are clauses which state restricted requirements of the shipment vessels, age of the vessels and the shipment route, etc..
	risks caused by taking - effect clauses: $X6$	(a) risks caused by the clauses such as "the L/C does not take effect for the time being"; " when the L/C takes effect is up to the bank's notification"; "the L/C will take effect upon the importer's receipt of payment from a third party"; "payment will be only made upon the approval by the Administration of Exchange Control after the arrival of the goods at the destination".
	risks caused by contradictory clauses: $X7$	The terms and conditions are contradictory, and the beneficiary can in no way achieve consistency among documents. E. g.: While it allows the submission of the combined transport B/L on the one hand, it on the other hand prohibits transshipment.
	risks caused by operation personnel: $X8$	risks brought by manager, salesman, paperwork operator, bank staff, and document examiner (forged L/C).
operation	risks caused by operation system: $X9$	risks caused by problems in the negotiation system, IT software system as well as the banks' electronic system.
	risks caused by the influences of external incidents: $X13$	settlement risks caused by changes in the external environment of L/C settlement, such as changes of political, economic and social environment.
	risks caused by changes of clients' credit: $X10$	risks caused by the changes of clients' trading history or changes of clients' assets and liabilities.
	risks caused by changes of legal environment: $X11$	risks caused by changes of UPC, quota restriction as well as policies and regulations of WTO.
	risks caused by changes of economic environment $X12$	risks caused by financial crisis, exchange rate problems, tax problems, the formation and development of economic community.

Table5-1(续)

1st level risk parameters	2nd level risk parameters	description and interpretation of the parameters
micro- or macro - environment	risks caused by changes of political environment : *X*14	risks caused by changes of leadership (president, prime minister, etc.) and change of the regional situation.
	risks caused by changes of cultural environment: *X*15	risks caused by shift of cultural environment from Anglo-American culture to Asian Confucian culture or to Islamic culture, etc..

Many researchers believe that there is a high degree of correlation and overlap among the parameter *X*13 (influences of external incidents), *X*12 (changes of economic environment) and *X*11 (changes of legal environment). Moreover, both *X*14 (risks caused by changes of political environment) and *X*15 (risks caused by changes of cultural environment) affect the L/C settlement through influencing *X*11 (risks caused by changes of legal environment) and *X*12 (risks caused by changes of economic environment). By secret ballot and several repeated tests with Delphi method, it is suggested that we cancel the three parameters including *X*13 (risks caused by the influences of external incidents), *X*14 (risks caused by changes of political environment) and *X*15 (risks caused by changes of cultural environment).

5.2.3 Exploratory Factor Analysis of L/C Risks

Questionnaires: A total of 300 questionnaires are distributed through e-mails or on-set, and 220 questionnaires are recovered. The recovery rate is 73%, which is in the range of valid value for it is much bigger than the required rate of 30%.

(1) KMO and Bartlett's spherical test: Use KMO to test the simple correlation coefficient and the partial correlation coefficient, and use Bartlett's spherical test to examine the distribution characteristics and the independence of the sample data. Using SPSS statistical software to analyze the data, the results are: (a) The value of KMO equals to 0.781, which is greater than 0.5 specified by Kaiser, indicating that it is feasible to carry out the factorial analysis; (b) the Chi - square value is 1 737.927, degree of freedom is 66, and the concomitant probability is 0 (smaller than 0.000 1). These values reject the hypothesis of variables being the identity matrix, indicating that they are suitable for factor analysis.

Table 5-2 Results of KMO and Bartlett's Spherical Test

KMO andBartlett's Test		
KMO Measurement of Sampling Adequacy		0. 781
Bartlett's Test of Sphericity	Approx. Chi-Square	1 737. 927
	df	66
	Sig.	0. 000

(2) Effect of common factor extraction: By analyzing the interrelation between variables and factors with SPSS, we can get the loading of each variable on each factor which indicates the correlation degree between the two. The larger the factor loading is, the higher the correlation degree will be. And generally speaking, if the factor loading is smaller than 0. 5, then it means that the correlation degree is not obvious and thus the related factor can be deleted. In this empirical study, by making a correlation matrix and doing the Eigen value extraction as well as rotating with the maximum variance method, factor loading matrix of table 5-3 is obtained. As can be seen from the table, the loading values of the variables *X*1, *X*2, *X*3, *X*4, *X*5, *X*6, *X*7 on the factor *F*1 are bigger than 0. 7, the loading values of the variables *X*10, *X*11, *X*12 on the factor *F*2 bigger than 0. 6, and the loading values of the variables *X*8, *X*9 on *F*3 bigger than 0. 7.

Table 5-3 Matrix of Factor Variance Loading

risk parameters	*F*1	*F*2	*F*3
risks caused by the contract clauses: *X*1	0. 894	0. 185	-0. 121
risks caused by the B/L clauses: *X*2	0. 868	0. 293	0. 047
risks caused by the signature and seal affixation clauses: *X*3	0. 932	0. 101	0. 130
risk caused by inspection clauses : *X*4	0. 809	0. 210	0. 286
risks caused by shipment clauses : *X*5	0. 910	0. 124	0. 133
risks caused by taking- effect clauses : *X*6	0. 815	0. 346	0. 234
risks caused by contradictory clauses : *X*7	0. 736	0. 427	0. 326
risks caused by operation personnel : *X*8	0. 139	0. 167	0. 791
risks caused by operation system : *X*9	0. 118	-0. 083	0. 914
risks caused by changes of clients' credit state : *X*10	0. 210	0. 900	0. 200

Table5-3(续)

risk parameters	*F*1	*F*2	*F*3
risks caused by changes of legal environment : *X*11	0. 183	0. 819	-0. 264
risks caused by changes of economic environment : *X*12	0. 410	0. 649	0. 298

(3) Extraction and nomenclature of the common factors.

Table 5-4 Eigen Values and Variance Contributions of the Factors

Total Variance Explained									
N	Initial Eigenvalues			Extraction Sums of Squared Loadings			Rotation Sums of Squared Loadings		
	Total	% of Variance	Cumulative %	Total	% of Variance	Cumulative %	Total	% of Variance	Cumulative %
1	6. 756	56. 296	56. 296	6. 756	56. 296	56. 296	5. 434	45. 286	45. 286
2	1. 667	13. 893	70. 189	1. 667	13. 893	70. 189	2. 406	20. 054	65. 340
3	1. 397	11. 639	81. 828	1. 397	11. 639	81. 828	1. 979	16. 488	81. 828
4	0. 602	5. 018	86. 846						
5	0. 416	3. 464	90. 310						
6	0. 286	2. 387	92. 697						
7	0. 281	2. 345	95. 041						
8	0. 196	1. 630	96. 671						
9	0. 174	1. 452	98. 123						
10	0. 116	0. 970	99. 093						
11	0. 069	0. 577	99. 671						
12	0. 040	0. 329	100. 00						

Extraction Method: Principal Component Analysis.

The Eigen value of the first common factor is 6. 756, and it turns into 5. 434 after rotation. Its variance contribution rate is 56. 296% before rotation and 45. 286% after rotation. The variables covered by the first common factor include risks caused by the B/L clauses, risks caused by the signature and seal affixation clauses, risks caused by the insurance clauses, risk caused by inspection clauses, risks caused by shipment clauses, risks caused by taking- effect clauses, as well as risks caused by contradictory clauses, which all belong to risks caused by the letter of credit itself. The Eigen value of the second common factor is 1. 667 and it turns into 2. 406 after rotation. Its variance contribution rate is 13. 893% before rotation and 20. 054% after rotation. The variables covered by the second common factor include risks caused by operation personnel and risks caused by operation system, which reflect the operational risks of banks, import and export enterprise personnel in the L/C operation process.

The Eigen value of the third common factor is 1. 397, and it turns into 1. 979 after rotation. Its variance contribution rate is 11. 639% before rotation and 16. 488% after rotation. The variables covered by the third common factor include risks caused by changes of clients' credit, risks caused by changes of legal environment and risks caused by changes of economic environment, which show the micro and the macro environmental risk factors in L/C settlement. The Eigen values of the three common factors are all bigger than 1 and the cumulative contribution rate is 81. 828, indicating that the three common factors *F*1, *F*2, *F*3 basically can reflect the information of all the parameters and the results are in accordance with the pre – formulated factor analysis model.

Nomenclature of the common factors: According to the variables included in the common factor *F*1, *F*1 can be renamed as clause risks; similarly, *F*2, operation risks; *F*3, environment risks (enterprise credit risks or national risks).

5. 3 SD Simulation Analysis of the L/C Risks

Based on the exploratory factor analysis of the L/C risk factors, the SD causes tree can be first constructed. Then, the risks are assessed and controlled through the SD simulation.

The traditional researches on risks of the L/C system mainly evaluate the L/C risks from the perspective of a single system such as the document system, the import and export commercial banking system, or the environment system and so on. Very few have had them combined to form a complex system for research. Fortunately, some shortcomings of these studies can be made up through SD studies.

Fig. 5-1 shows the general process of SD simulation which regards system as a multi-layer information feedback system. In SD simulation, the researchers can first make an in-depth analysis of the system which will then be decomposed into different factor sets. After that, these factor sets will be linked up to establish the causes feedback tree. Later, the system flow chart will be set up with the Vensim software (including the establishment and input of the dynamo equation). Finally, simulation experiment of the real system structure will be conducted to find out the optimal system structure.

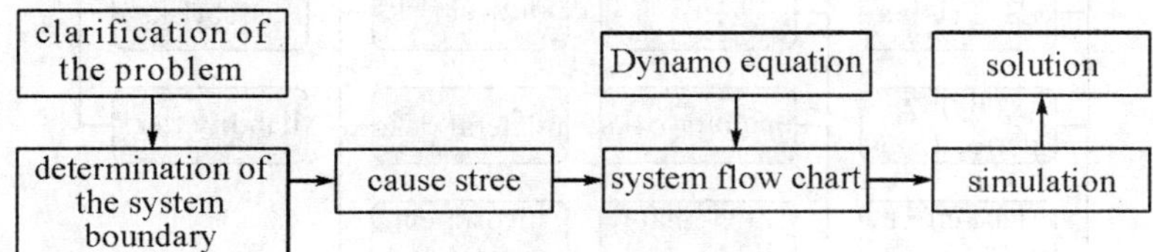

Fig. 5-1 **SD Flow Chart**

5.3.1 Model design and parameter setting

5.3.1.1 CausesTree Design for L/C Settlement Risks in International Trade

(1) clarification of the problem.

The assessment system of L/C settlement risks is a complex system, which in accordance with the results of the exploratory factor analysis, can be divided into four subsystems: the subsystem of national risks, the subsystem of enterprise credit risks, the subsystem of operation risks, and the subsystem of clause risks. And each of these subsystems can also be further divided into several sub-subsystems, mainly including the country state risk system, political risk system, economic state risk system, investment state risk system, bilateral relationship risk system, operation process risk system, operator risk system, operation system risk system, external event risk system, moral hazard system, liability risk system, asset risk system, the validity period risk system, document presentation date risk system, the shipment time risk system, the inspection risk system, the B/L risk system, the take-effect condition risk system, as well as the terms of payment risk system, etc..

We can understand the relationship among the various factors through the following fig.:

From Fig. 5-2, we can clearly see the logical relationships among the L/C risks on hierarchies A to C, and the factors on different hierarchies are linked up by functions.

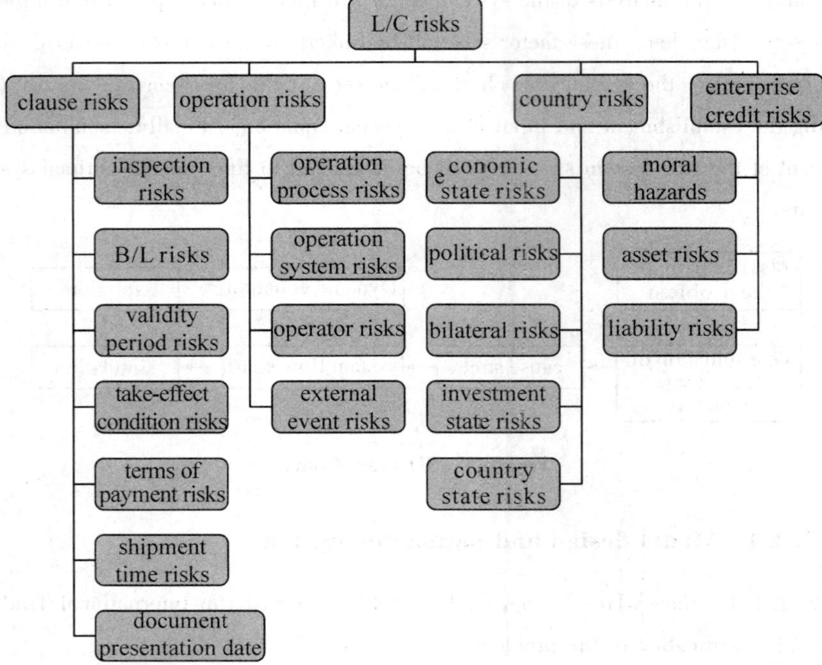

Fig. 5-2 Relationship among Factors on Hierarchies A to C

Similarly, from Fig. 5-3 we can clearly see the logical relationships among the L/C risks on hierarchies B to D. Again, the factors and hierarchies are linked up by functions.

(2) Secondly, draw the causes tree of L/C settlement risks according to the cause and effect relationship obtained from the target problem, paying attention to the interaction between factors and the polarity characteristics of the positive and negative poles.

From Fig. 5-4, we can clearly see the construction characteristics of the entire factors system for the L/C settlement risks. At the same time, we can also see the interaction principle of the factors and the polar relationship among the factors.

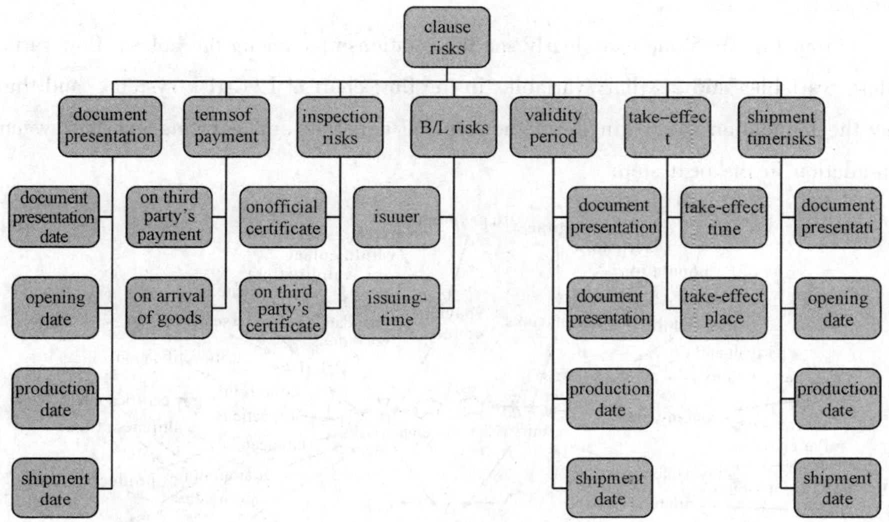

Fig. 5-3 Relationship among Factors on Hierarchies B to D (Taking Clause Risks as an Example)

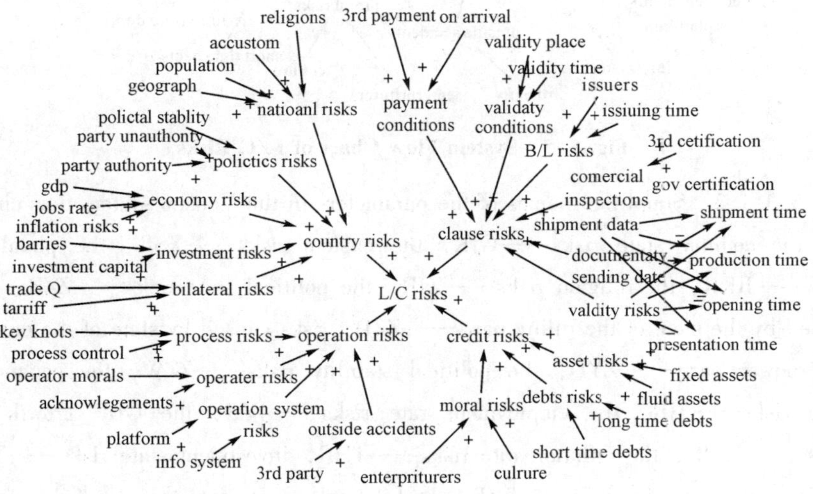

Fig. 5-4 Causes Tree of the L/C Risk System

5.3.1.2 Drawing the system flow chart based on the causes tree of L/C settlement risks with Vensim

Through the causes tree, the relationships between variables are sorted out, and the risk factors are organically linked up with holes, flow variables, variables, auxiliary variables, etc.

From Fig. 5-5 one can clearly see the relationships among the holes, flow variables, variables and auxiliary variables in the flow chart of L/C risk system, and thus lay the foundation for writingdown the dynamo equation and carrying out the system simulation in the next step.

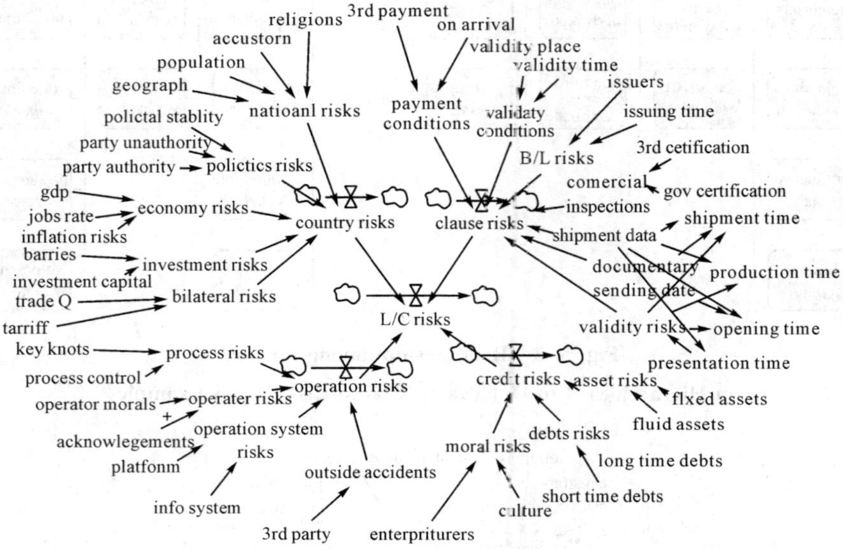

Fig. 5-5 System Flow Chart of L/C Risks

5.3.1.3 Simplified names of the parameters in the Vensim system flow chart

the country state risks——GJK, the custom risks——XSR, the population risks——RKR, the religion risks——ZJR, the political state risks——ZZR, risks caused by the state of the ruling party——ZZD, risks caused by state of the out-of-the-power party——ZYD, the political stability risks——ZZW, the economical state risks——JJR, the employment rate risks——JYR, the GDP growth rate risks——GDPR, the inflation rate risks——THR, investment state risks——TZZ, the investment barrier risks——TZB, the bilateral investment amount risks——SBT, the trade risks——JMG, the trade barrier risks——MYB, the bilateral trade amount risks——SBM, the asset risks——ZCR, the fixed asset risks——GDR, the current asset risks——LDR, the liability risks——FZR, the long-term liability risks——CQR, the short-term liability risks——DQR, the moral hazards——DDR, the enterprise culture risks——QYW, the entrepreneur quality risks——QQJ, the terms of payment risks——FKT, risks caused by the requirement of being on the third party's payment——DSF, risks caused by the arrival of cargo requirement——HDF, the take-effect condition risks——SXT, the take-effect place requirement risks——SXD, the take-effect time requirement risks——SXS, the B/L risks——TDF, the B/L issuing date risks——TDR, the B/L issuer risks——TDC, the inspection risks——SJF, the official inspection certificate risks——GFS, the third party inspection certificate risks——DSF, the shipment preparation period risks——ZCQ, the validity period risks——YXQ, the document preparation period risks——JDQ, the production time risks——SCR, the opening risks——KZR, the shipment date risks——ZCR, the document presentation date risks——JDR, the operation process risks——CZL, the process control risks——LCK, the process node risks——LCJ, the operator risks——CZR, the moral quality risks——DDP, the professional quality risks——YWS, the external event risks——WBS, the third party event risks——DSS, the operation system risks——CZX, the operation platform risks——CZP, the information system risks——XXX, the national risks——GJR, the enterprise credit risks——QYC, the clause risks——TKR, the operation risks——CZR, the L/C risks——XYZ.

5.3.1.4 Writing the corresponding dynamo equations based on the quantitative relationship within the system flow chart

$$GJK = XSR \times a1 + RKR \times b1 + ZJR \times c1 \quad (5.1)$$

$$ZZR = ZZD \times a2 + ZYD \times b2 + ZJW \times c2 \quad (5.2)$$

$$JJR = JYR \times a3 + GDPR \times b3 + THR \times c3 \quad (5.3)$$

$$TZZ = TZB \times a4 + SBT \times b4 \quad (5.4)$$

$$JMG = MYB \times a5 + SBM \times b5 \quad (5.5)$$

$$ZCR = GDR \times a6 + LDR \times b6 \quad (5.6)$$

$$FZR = CQR \times a7 + DQR \times b7 \quad (5.7)$$

$$DDR = QYW \times a8 + QQJ \times b8 \quad (5.8)$$

$$FKT = DSF \times a9 + HDF \times b9 \quad (5.9)$$

$$SXT = SXD \times a10 + SXS \times b10 \quad (5.10)$$

$$TDF = TDR \times a11 + TDC \times b11 \quad (5.11)$$

$$SJF = GFS \times a12 + DSF \times b12 \quad (5.12)$$

$$ZCQ = SCR \times a13 + KZR \times b13 + ZCR \times c13 + JDR \times d13 \quad (5.13)$$

$$YXQ = SCR \times a14 + KZR \times b14 + ZCR \times c14 + JDR \times d14 \quad (5.14)$$

$JDQ = SCR \times a15 + KZR \times b15 + ZCR \times c15 + JDR \times d15$ (5.15)

$CZL = LCK \times a16 + LCJ \times b16$ (5.16)

$CZR = DDP \times a17 + YWS \times b17$ (5.17)

$WBS = DSS \times a18$ (5.18)

$CZX = CZP \times a19 + XXX \times b19$ (5.19)

$GJR = GJK \times e1 + ZZR \times f1 + JJR \times g1 + TZZ \times h1 + JMG \times i1$ (5.20)

$QYC = ZCR \times e2 + FZR \times f2 + DDR \times g2$ (5.21)

$TKR = FKT \times e3 + SXT \times f3 + TDF \times g3 + SJF \times h3 + ZCQ \times i3 + YXQ \times j3 + JDQ \times k3$ (5.22)

$CZR = CZL \times e4 + CZR \times f4 + WBS \times g4 + CZX \times h4$ (5.23)

$XYZ = GJR \times L + QYC \times M + TKR \times N + CZR \times O$ (5.24)

($e1$, $e2$, $e3$…; $f1$, $f2$, $f3$…; $g1$, $g2$, $g3$…; $h1$, $h2$, $h3$…; $i1$, $i2$, $i3$…; $j1$, $j2$, $j3$…; $k1$, $k2$, $k3$…; L, M, N here are the weights of the parameters)

5.3.2 Simulation Analysis of System Model

5.3.2.1 Assumptions of the System Model

To have a clear sense of the fluctuations in the L/C settlement risk system, we simplify the system and bring out some assumptions.

(1) Assume that participants in the L/C settlement system are all rational economic persons, and they are all in the pursuit of the payoff maximization under equal risk conditions.

(2) Suppose that the initial target values for the parameters in the L/C settlement sub-systems and on their corresponding lower levels are all 0 except that the fluctuations of three factors (the ruling party state risks, the political stability risks and the short-term liability risks) conform to different distributions.

5.3.2.2 Simulation Analysis of the L/C settlement risk system

Carry out the simulation analysis with a computer:

Initial settings:

FINAL TIME = 100

Units: Month

The final time for the simulation

INITIAL TIME = 0

Units: Month

The final time for the simulation

SAVEPER = TIME STEP

Units: Month [0, 100]

The frequency with which output is stored

Time STEP = 1

Units: Month [0, 100]

The time step for simulation

From the above 4 figures (Fig. 5-6~Fig. 5-9) it can be seen that the fluctuations of risk factors on hierarchy D —fluctuation of the ruling party state risk and fluctuation of the political stability risks—conform to different distributions, and their interaction will result in the fluctuation of the risk factor on hierarchy C—fluctuation of political state risks. What's more, the fluctuation patterns of the risk factor on hierarchy B—the national risk, the risk factor on hierarchy C—political state risks and the risk factors on hierarchy D —the ruling party state risks and the political stability risks—are similar to some extent (only to some extent, though): they are similar for they have some internal connections. however, they are also different for they have different fluctuation amplitudes and peaks . This indicates that the system risks are influenced by both the agglomeration effect and the dispersion effect.

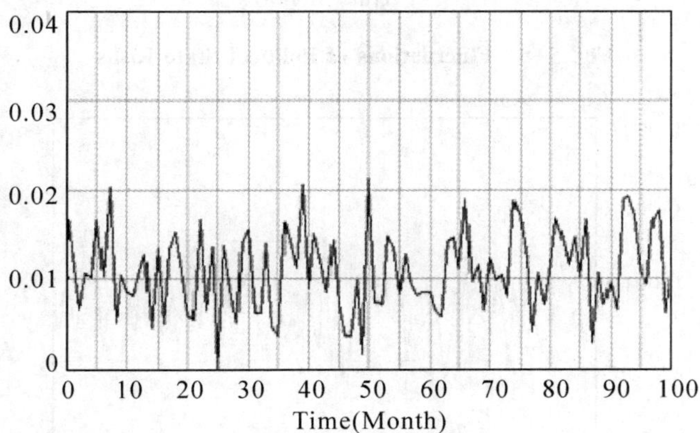

Fig. 5-6 Fluctuations of the Ruling Party State Risks

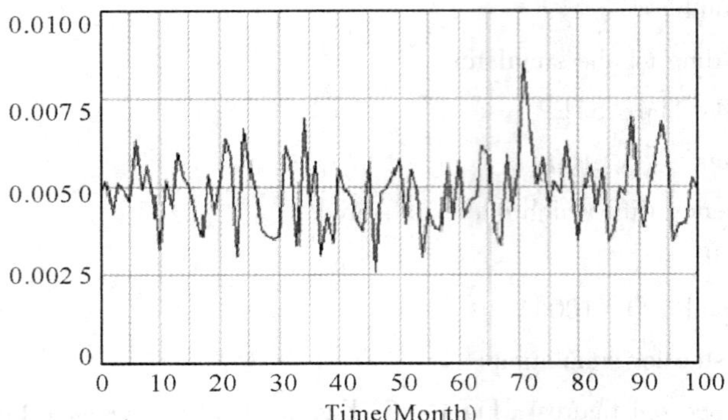

Fig. 5-7 Fluctuations of the Political Stability Risks

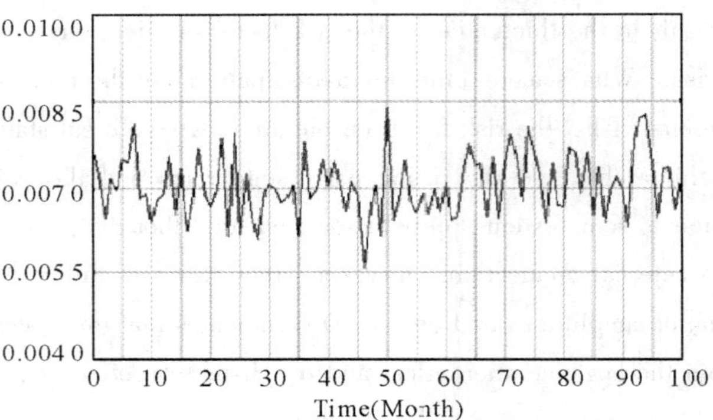

Fig. 5-8 Fluctuations of Political State Risks

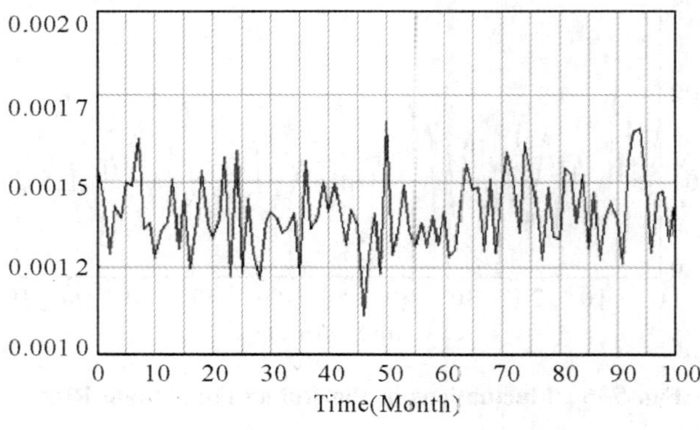

Fig. 5-9 Fluctuations of National Risks

From the above 4 figures (Fig. 5-10~Fig. 5-13) it can be seen that fluctuation of the hierarchy D risk factor—short-term liability risks will affect fluctuation of the enterprise credit risks which will then affect the fluctuation of the hierarchy A risk factor— L/C risks. Their fluctuation patterns are sometimes similar and sometimes different (they have quite obvious differences especially in the fluctuation amplitude and peak). Based on the fluctuation of the hierarchy A risk factor —L/C risks, system risk analysts can determine the risk control time by observing the peak areas of the system. For example, the peak values may appear at the 7th month, the 20th month, the27th month, the 37th month, the 43rd month, the 60th month, the 68th month, the 76th month, the 82rd month, the 89th month, the 92rd month, the 95th month and so on. Thus, on these nodes, the enterprises or the financial institutions should be prepared for risk prevention in advance.

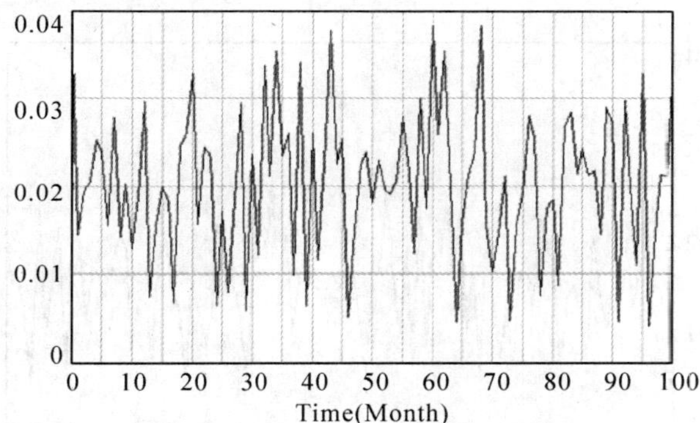

Fig. 5-10 Fluctuations of Short-Term Liability Risks

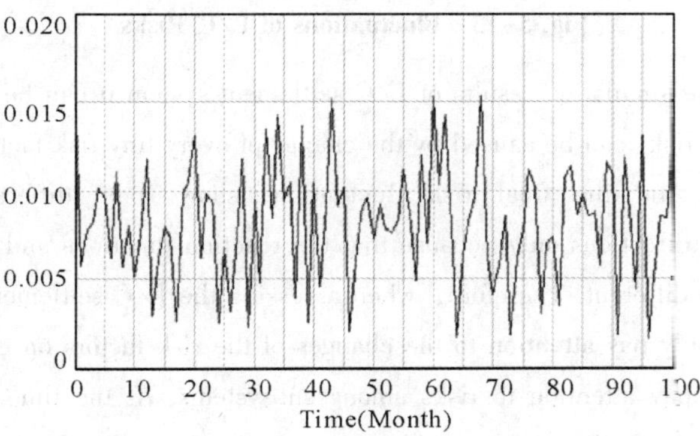

Fig. 5-11 Fluctuations of Liability Risks

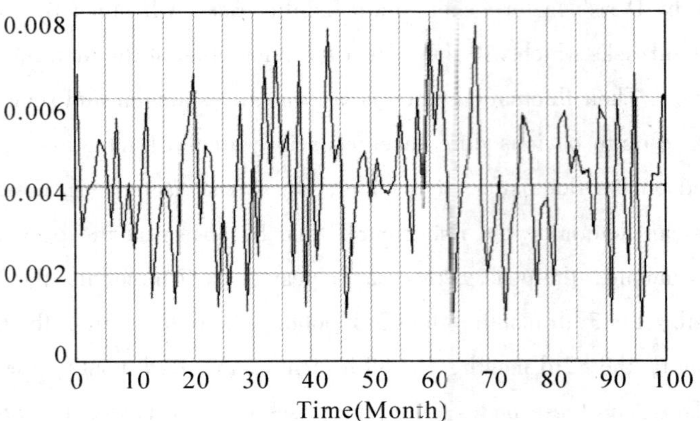

Fig. 5-12 Fluctuations of Enterprise Credit Risks

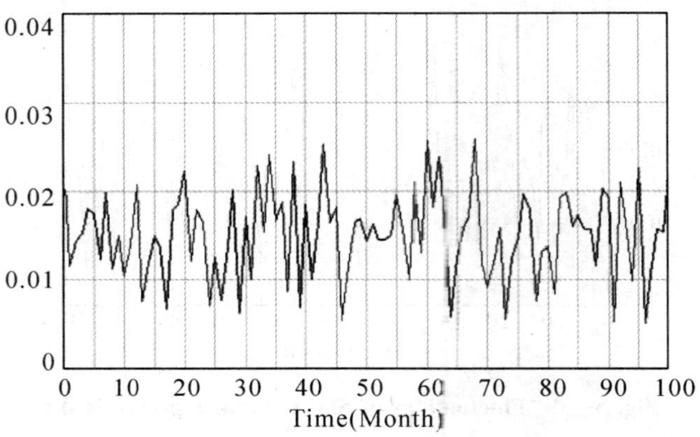

Fig. 5-13 Fluctuations of L/C Risks

Through the simulation results of L/C settlement system it can be seen that fluctuations of L/C risks can be caused by the change of every tiny risk factor on each system hierarchy. And the final risk fluctuations show some differences in their magnitudes and directions only because that the reaction functions and the conduction mechanisms are different. Therefore, when assessing the L/C settlement risk system, we should not only pay attention to the changes of the risk factors on each hierarchy, but also should pay attention to risks among subsystems. At the time when the L/C risk is about to reach the peak, we should take a variety of measures to have them prevented and controlled. For instance, we can adopt some export- credit- insurance based methods to prevent L/C settlement risks so as to ensure that the systemic risks can be effectively controlled when occur.

5.4 Conclusions

No one can deny that L/C has many advantages in international settlements. However, it also has some bottlenecks such as relatively complex application method, difficult risk assessment techniques and high risk control requirements. Based on and instead of the previous qualitative researches, the quantitative research method is adopted in this study. It first extracts the common factors of L/C settlement risks with the method of exploratory factor analysis. After that, it constructs the SD simulation model, through which it studies the fluctuations of the L/C risks under different parameters. Next, it observes the peak values of the L/C settlement risks through the simulation model, after which it also brings about the method for timely and effectively preventing and controlling the possible L/C settlement risks.

参考文献

[1] MODIGLIANI F, MILLER M H. The Cost of Capital, Corporation Finance and the Theory of Investment [J]. American Economic Review, 1958, 48 (6): 261— 297.

[2] STIGLITZ J E. On the Irrelevance of Corporate Financial Policy [J]. American Economic Review, 1974, 64 (6): 851-866.

[3] WARNER J B. On Financial Contracting: An Analysis of Bond Covenants [J]. Journal of Financial Economics, 1979, 7 (2): 117-161.

[4] TIMAN S, WESSELS R. The Determinants of Capital Structure Choice [J]. Journal of Finance, 1988, 43 (1): 1-19.

[5] JENSEN M C, MECKLING W H. Theory of the Firm: Managerial Behavior, Agency Costs and Ownership Structure [J]. Journal of Financial Economics, 1976 (3): 305-360.

[6] ROSS S A. The Determination of Financial Structure: The Incentive Signalling Approach [J]. Bell Journal of Economics, 1977, 8 (1): 23-40.

[7] PYLE D H, LELAND H E. Information Asymmetries, Financial Structure, and Financial Intermediation [J]. Journal of Finance, 1977, 32 (2): 371-387.

[8] MYERS S C, MAJLUF N S. Corporate Financing and Investment Decisions When Firms Have Information that Investors Do Not Have [J]. Journal of Financial Economics, 1984, 13 (2): 187-221.

[9] STULZ R. Managerial Control of Voting Rights: Financing Policies and the Market for Corporate Control [J]. Journal of Financial Economics, 1988, 20 (1-2): 25-54.

[10] ISRAEL R. Capital Structure and the Market for Corporate Control: The Defensive Role of Debt Financing [J]. Journal of Finance, 1991, 46 (4): 1 391-

1 409.

[11] HART O, MOORE J. Default and Renegotiation: A Dynamic Model of Debt [J]. Quartely Journal of Economics, 1998, 113 (1): 1-41.

[12] MASULIS R W. The Impact of Capital Structure Change on Firm Value: Some Estimates [J]. Journal of Finance, 1983, 38 (1): 107-126.

[13] VERMAELEN T. Common Stock Repurchase and Market Signalling [J]. Journal of Financial Economies, 1981, 9 (2) .

[14] TAGOE N, AMARH E A, NYARKO E. SME Access to Bank Finance in an Emerging Economy: The Role of Information Management Practices [J]. International Journal of Financial Services Management, 2008, 3 (2): 148-170.

[15] POPESCU, CRISTIAN-AURELIAN. ConsiderationsRegarding SME's Access to Finance [J]. UPB Scientific Bulletin, Series D: Mechanical Engineering, 2008, 70 (1): 97-106.

[16] IRWIN D, SCOTT J M. Barriers Faced by SMEs in Raising Bank Finance [J]. International Journal of Entrepreneurial Behavior & Research, 2010, 16 (3): 245-259.

[17] KUNDID A, ERCEGOVAC R. Credit Rationing in Financial Distress: Croatia SMEs' Finance Approach [J]. International Journal of Law & Management, 2011, 53 (1): 62-84.

[18] STEPHENS, KEN. Quality Principles, Philosophies, and Methodologies Applicable to the Mortgage-Finance Supply Chain [J]. Quality Management Journal, 2009, 16 (3): 26-27.

[19] ZIPKIN P. Quality Snags in the Mortgage-Finance Supply Chain [J]. Quality Management Journal, 2009, 16 (3): 7-18.

[20] WATTKE D A, BLOME C, HENKE M. Focusing the Financial Flow of Supply Chains: An Empirical Investigation of Financial Supply Chain Management [J]. International Journal of Production Economics, 2013, 145 (2): 773-789.

[21] CHEN T K, LIAO H H, KUO H J. Internal Liquidity Risk, Financial Bullwhip Effects, and Corporate Bond Yield Spreads: Supply Chain Perspectives [J]. Journal of Banking & Fianance, 2013, 37 (7): 2 434-2 456.

[22] CHARLES F. Innovations in Supply Chain Finance Technology and Financing Helping Companies Gain Cost Advantages [J]. Automotive Industries, 2006, 186 (9): 16-18.

[23] BASU P, NAIR S K. Supply Chain Finance Enabled Early Pay: Unlocking Trapped Value in B2B Logistics [J]. International Journal of Logistics Systems & Management, 2012, 12 (3): 334-353.

[24] MORE D, BASU P. Challenges of Supply Chain Finance: a Detailed Study and a Hierarchical Model Based on the Experiences of an Indian Firm [J]. Business Process Management Journal, 2013, 9 (4): 624-647.

[25] ALAVI H. Contractual Restrictions on Right of Beneficiary to Draw on a Letter of Credit: Possible Exception to Principle of Autonomy [J]. International and Comparative Law Review, 2016.

[26] ALAVI H. Limits of Autonomy Principle in Documentary Letters of Credit: Perspective of English Law [J]. Journal of Legal Studies, 2017.

[27] SUSMUS T, BASLANGIC S O. The New Payment Term BPO and Its Effects on Turkish International Business [J]. Procedia Economics & Finance, 2015 (33): 321-330.

[28] ALAVI H. Mitigating the Risk of Fraud in Documentary Letters of Credit [J]. Baltic Journal of European Studies, 2016.

[29] NIEPMANN F, SCHMIDT-EISENLOHR T. No Guarantees, No Trade: How Banks Affect Export Patterns [J]. Journal of International Economics, 2017 (108): 338-350.

[30] CHEHASHIM R. Fraudin Letter of Credit Transactions: the Experience of Malaysian Bankers [J]. International Journal of Law Crime & Justice, 2014, 42 (3): 224-236.

[31] NIEPMANN F, SCHMIDT-EISENLOHR T. International Trade, Risk and the Role of Banks [J]. Journal of International Economics, 2017 (107): 111-126.

[32] 许家林，胡汇杰. 负债融资：观念的确立及推进举措 [J]. 中国软科学, 2003 (6): 56-60.

[33] 杨兴全，陈旭东. 企业负债融资与产品市场竞争 [J]. 经济管理, 2004 (6): 9-15.

[34] 杨兴全，陈旭东. 负债融资契约的治理效应分析 [J]. 财政研究, 2004 (8): 53-56.

[35] 吴昊，武央，邓宜康. 委托—代理关系下企业的筹资决策研究 [J]. 数量经济技术经济研究, 2004, 21 (4): 92-95.

[36] 邵国良，王满四. 上市公司负债融资的股权结构效应实证分析 [J]. 中国软科学，2005 (3)：61-66.

[37] 周振红，黄深泽. 企业激励机制与筹资决策分析 [J]. 统计与决策，2006 (9)：128-129.

[38] 吴春雷，马林梅. 上市公司最佳资本结构：基于财务预警的实证研究 [J]. 经济纵横，2007 (20)：23-25.

[39] 郑瑞玺，徐新华，何青. 股东套利行为与企业融资方式选择 [J]. 中央财经大学学报，2007 (2)：32-38.

[40] 戴钰. 我国上市公司负债融资的治理效应研究 [J]. 湖南大学学报 (社会科学版)，2011 (1)：57-62.

[41] 刘凤良，连洪泉. 产品市场竞争策略和公司负债融资决策 [J]. 商业经济与管理，2012 (2)：44-52.

[42] 穆玉堂. 我国金融资本流动绩效评价 [J]. 经济问题，2013 (7)：61-66.

[43] 宋小保. 最终控制人、负债融资与利益侵占：来自中国民营上市公司的经验证据 [J]. 系统工程理论与实践，2014，34 (7)：1 633-1 641.

[44] 何瑛，张大伟. 管理者特质、负债融资与企业价值 [J]. 会计研究，2015 (8)：65-72.

[45] 王希胜. 负债融资与公司绩效实证研究——基于终极控制人的视角 [J]. 河南社会科学，2015 (6)：76-80.

[46] 王昌荣，马红，王元月. 基于宏观经济政策视角的我国企业负债融资研究 [J]. 中国管理科学，2016，24 (5)：158-167.

[47] 黄小琳，朱松，陈关亭. 持股金融机构对企业负债融资与债务结构的影响——基于上市公司的实证研究 [J]. 金融研究，2015 (12)：130-145.

[48] 朱佳俊，周方召. 市场份额、负债融资与企业价值——基于中国房地产上市公司的实证研究 [J]. 技术经济，2017，36 (1)：117-122.

[49] 陈涛，党兴华，贾宾洁，等. 互联网企业负债融资对技术效率的动态耦合效应 [J]. 科研管理，2016，37 (12)：132-143.

[50] 孙婷，宋志彬. 温州民间借贷问题的研究 [J]. 中国证券期货，2011 (12)：139.

[51] 朱振球. 民间借贷趋势分析与风险防范策略研究 [J]. 金融经济，2009 (10)：70-71.

[52] 张东琴，叶艺超. 金融危机对我国出口企业的影响 [J]. 中国证券期货，2011 (7)：167.

[53] 陈大艳. 苏州中小出口企业国际贸易融资问题探析 [J]. 苏州科技学院学报（社会科学版），2009，26（2）：19-22.

[54] 陈宁，林汉川. 后危机时代广东中小出口企业面临的困境及对策 [J]. 特区经济，2010（6）：41-42.

[55] 郑熙春. 欧债危机下我国出口企业的困境及应对对策探讨 [J]. 现代商贸工业，2012，24（3）：73-74.

[56] 闫俊宏，许祥秦. 基于供应链金融的中小企业融资模式分析 [J]. 上海金融，2007（2）：14-16.

[57] 陈李宏，彭芳春. 供应链金融——中小企业融资新途径 [J]. 湖北社会科学，2008（11）：101-103.

[58] 余剑梅. 以供应链金融缓解中小企业融资难问题 [J]. 经济纵横，2011（3）：99-102.

[59] 胡跃飞，黄少卿. 供应链金融：背景、创新与概念界定 [J]. 财经问题研究，2009（8）：76-82.

[60] 彭柳洁. 供应链金融模式下商业银行对中小企业授信问题研究 [D]. 广州：暨南大学，2008.

[61] 赵亚娟，杨喜孙，刘心报. 供应链金融与中小企业信贷能力的提升 [J]. 金融理论与实践，2009（10）：46-51.

[62] 张浩. 基于供应链金融的中小企业信用评级模型研究 [J]. 东南大学学报（哲学社会科学版），2008，10（S2）：54-58.

[63] 汪守国，徐莉. 供应链融资模型及其风险分析 [J]. 商业时代，2009（22）：75-76.

[64] 熊熊，马佳，赵文杰，等. 供应链金融模式下的信用风险评价 [J]. 南开管理评论，2009，12（4）：92-98.

[65] 时广静. 基于供应链金融的契约协调研究 [D]. 成都：西南交通大学，2008.

[66] 弯红地. 供应链金融的风险模型分析研究 [J]. 经济问题，2008（11）：109-112.

[67] 王琪. 基于决策树的供应链金融模式信用风险评估 [J]. 新金融，2010（4）：38-41.

[68] 周学农. 供应链金融管理 [J]. 系统工程，2010（8）：85-88.

[69] 何宜庆，郭婷婷. 供应链融资模式下中小企业融资行为的博弈模型分析 [J]. 南昌大学学报（工科版），2010，32（2）：183-187.

[70] 徐岩，胡斌，钱任. 基于随机演化博弈的战略联盟稳定性分析和仿真 [J]. 系统工程理论与实践，2011，31（5）：920-926.

[71] 乔晓宇. 供应链金融模式下成本收益的博弈分析 [J]. 商业经济，2011（22）：28-31.

[72] 李雯靓. 基于多主体的供应链金融信用风险博弈仿真研究 [D]. 广州：华南理工大学，2012.

[73] 杨晏忠. 论商业银行供应链金融的风险防范 [J]. 金融论坛，2007，12（10）：42-45.

[74] 田雷，刘文笑. 商业银行供应链金融业务研究 [J]. 金融经济，2011（3）：60-62.

[75] 周纯敏. 商业银行对供应链融资的风险管理 [J]. 山西财经大学学报，2009，31（S2）：115-116.

[76] 仉瑄，李海鹏. 商业银行交易链融资业务的授信模式与风险控制 [J]. 新金融，2011（4）：46-47.

[77] 白少布，刘洪. 基于供应链保兑仓融资的企业风险收益合约研究 [J]. 软科学，2009，23（10）：118-122.

[78] 甄莹，芦玮. 如何在钢材贸易中规范操作保兑仓业务 [J]. 中国物流与采购，2009（23）：54-55.

[79] 史丽媛，叶蜀君. 仓单质押与保兑仓模式增值机理分析 [J]. 金融与经济，2010（10）：69-71.

[80] 房艳蕾，张义刚. 使用保兑仓进行采购的意义 [J]. 中国物流与采购，2010（4）：70-71.

[81] 王超. 从保兑仓角度研究供应链金融 [J]. 金融经济，2011（10）：60-62.

[82] 钟佳萌. 保兑仓模式下零售商订购决策研究 [J]. 物流工程与管理，2012，34（1）：87-89.

[83] 林强，李晓征，师杰. 保兑仓融资模式下数量折扣契约的参数设计 [J]. 天津大学学报（社会科学版），2014，16（1）：12-17.

[84] 王珍. 浅谈太钢不锈开展保兑仓业务及其风险控制 [J]. 会计之友，2009（36）：62-63.

[85] 郭胜圣. 供应链金融的保兑仓决策研究 [D]. 北京：清华大学，2011.

[86] 杜永斌. 商业银行保兑仓业务信用风险防范研究 [D]. 武汉：华中

科技大学，2011.

［87］王儒泉. 保兑仓产品的风险研究［D］. 北京：北京交通大学，2013.

［88］任慧军，李智慧，方毅. 物流金融下保兑仓模式中的风险分析［J］. 物流技术，2013，32（7）：24-26.

［89］颜明，王军，张继霞，等. 基于 VaR 的保兑仓部分承诺回购模式研究［J］. 青岛大学学报（自然科学版），2013，26（2）：91-94.

［90］吴泽莹. 基于供应链金融的保兑仓参与方策略与风险评价研究［D］. 重庆：重庆大学，2014 .

［91］王玉珏. 透视利用信用证打包贷款实施诈骗的行为——兼论信用证诈骗本体行为模式［J］. 新疆社会科学，2012（3）：83-88.

［92］杜庆霞. 商业银行信用证融资业务风险控制探究［J］. 财会通讯，2014（8）：102-105.

［93］陈寰，林晓慧. 大宗商品贸易项下进口信用证业务的风险与控制——基于进口地银行的视野［J］. 对外经贸实务，2017（1）：57-60.

［94］南舒. 基于 BP 神经网络方法构建银行信用证风险评估模型［D］. 杭州：浙江理工大学，2017.

［95］封文丽. 信用证"软条款"及其风险防范［J］. 金融经济，2012（12）：75-77.

［96］王楚楚，周戈，王皓田. 国际结算业务中的诈骗风险防范及举例分析［J］. 对外经贸实务，2013（7）：72-74.

［97］周凌轲，黄颖，王普玉. 国际贸易背景下信用证软条款的理论识别方法［J］. 中国商论，2018（14）：67-68.

［98］林璇华. 信用证结算中我国出口商面临的风险及防范［J］. 长春理工大学学报（社会科学版），2013（5）：83-84.

［99］李晓蕾. 国际结算风险及防范研究［D］. 北京：首都经济贸易大学，2018.

［100］姜爱丽，王靖靖. UCP600 规则下我国针对信用证欺诈的立法完善［J］. 山东大学学报（哲学社会科学版），2012（6）：35-40.

［101］代兴军. 信用证欺诈例外及法律适用研究［J］. 国际金融，2012（5）：75-80.

［102］张晓微，姚新超. 信用证下部分装运与分期装运辨析—兼论 UCP600 第 31 条和第 32 条的适用［J］. 兰州大学学报（社会科学版），2016（6）：116-122.

[103] 沈四宝，蒋琪. 信用证出口押汇最新法律问题研究 [J]. 法学论坛，2018，33 (3)：98-108.

[104] 廖起平. 国际结算及贸易融资之全面电子化 [J]. 国际金融，2014 (6)：28-33.

[105] 王永梅. Z 银行信用证电子交单风险控制问题及优化方案研究 [D]. 上海：华东理工大学，2016.

[106] 中信银行上线国内首个区块链信用证信息传输系统 [J]. 中国金融电脑，2017 (8)：95.

[107] 张鹏. 区块链技术对商业银行传统贸易结算方式的影响研究 [D]. 北京：对外经济贸易大学，2017.

[108] 李丽琼. 探讨区块链技术冲击信用证商业银行的应对与管理 [D]. 昆明：云南财经大学，2017.

[109] 闵敢. 论我国出口企业信用证风险防范 [J]. 生产力研究，2007，17 (24)：122-123.

[110] 张守红. 信用证风险管理研究 [D]. 北京：北京交通大学，2008.

[111] 凌智. 国际贸易中跟单信用证风险与防范 [D]. 北京：首都经济贸易大学，2008.

[112] 李蕴萍. 建行大连分行出口信用证风险防范研究 [D]. 大连：大连理工大学，2009.

[113] 李楠. 金融危机背景下西安出口企业信用证风险及防范研究 [D]. 西安：西安理工大学，2010.